REVEALED

WHAT THE BIBLE
CAN TEACH YOU
ABOUT YOURSELF

ANGELA D. SCHAFFNER

UPPER
ROOM BOOKS®
NASHVILLE

For Dusty

Cover Design: Jay Smith, Juicebox Designs
Interior design and typesetting: PerfecType | Nashville, TN

Library of Congress Cataloging-in-Publication Data
    Names: Schaffner, Angela D., author.
    Title: Revealed : what the Bible can teach you about yourself / Angela D. Schaffner.
    Description: Nashville : Upper Room Books, 2019. | Includes bibliographical references.
    Identifiers: LCCN 2018042152 (print) | LCCN 2018056363 (ebook) | ISBN 9780835818629 (Mobi) | ISBN 9780835818636 (Epub) | ISBN 9780835818612 (print)
    Subjects: LCSH: Bible--Psychology. | Self--Biblical teaching.
    Classification: LCC BS645 (ebook) | LCC BS645 .S33 2019 (print) | DDC 220.601/9--dc23
    LC record available at https://lccn.loc.gov/2018042152

CONTENTS

ACKNOWLEDGMENTS

I am beyond grateful for the many people who contributed to the creation of this book. Kristen E. Vincent initially connected me with Joanna Bradley so I could propose my idea for this book to Upper Room Books. The team at The Upper Room transformed the original manuscript into a polished final version. I am especially thankful for Erin Palmer, my editor. Her expertise, insight and understanding of what I wanted to convey helped me communicate my stories so much more clearly and effectively.

Dusty showed great patience in reading drafts, providing honest feedback, and encouraging me to make time for writing. Jaime Blandino encouraged me to be a more honest and courageous version of myself, and that flowed into my writing. Michelle O'Donnell provided retreats in her quiet house in Hapeville, and her company repeatedly restored my sense of balance and peace. Danielle Veader walked with me through many conversations and challenges with family, parenting, and faith, always remaining a steady rock of support, making me laugh, and reminding me of the parts of life that are worth taking seriously and those that need to be let go. Erin Hurst is a source of steady support, kindness, and creative ideas. Rev. Susan Allen Grady is a mentor in ministry, friend, and writing companion who also provided valuable feedback on this book.

Many others gave insight on my early drafts as well, including Rebecca Cochran, the Rev. Dr. Glenn Ethridge, the Rev. Dr. Joseph McBrayer, the Rev. Dr. Amy Morgan, Brooke Peck, Rebecca Peet, Kristy Shackelford, and Melissa Youngren. Rebecca and Rebecca invited me to speak on their Woven podcast and cheered me on in my pursuit of getting this book published.

My therapist Dr. Debbara Dingman helped me look within myself so that I could look beyond myself. Master Mast and everyone at Atlanta's United Taekwondo showed me how to spar and break through obstacles with others' support. Our Taekwondo classes and post-kicking Thinking Man visits were just as good as therapy. *Taeguek sa jang!*

The Rev. Dr. Dana Everhart provided guidance when I explored a call to ministry, and my pastors at Oak Grove United Methodist Church provided especially excellent examples of how to live out faith with consistency and love, along with the entire staff who work as a cohesive team to serve the community of Oak Grove.

The ACE team, especially Dr. Linda Buchanan and Dr. Rick Kilmer, helped me develop professionally as we worked side by side for over twelve years helping people with eating disorders find lasting recovery. Every client I've worked with has touched my life and informed my writing and insights into the many paths through the complex dynamics of eating disorders and emotional pain. Dr. David Dixon and Dr. Donald Nicholas were mentors during my graduate school training who guided my development as a psychologist.

The Ladies of Leafmore inspired fun and singing and demonstrated the power of a supportive neighborhood community. Jessica Bandy, Marsey Devoto, Johnna Field, Kristi Gage, Allison Houston, Celia Henson, Martha McGourk, Hollie Meglio, Libby Parris, and Neisha Wagner studied and made sense of the Bible with me, prayed with me, and remain solid examples of living out faith in loving action.

Even at such young ages, my sons Carlson (11), Caleb (8) and Zach (5) seemed to sense how important this project was to me and consistently expressed excitement and joy about it. My dad encouraged me to do what I love, and my mom modeled the ability to make time for reading and writing while working, parenting, and volunteering. My sister, Elise, modeled the ability to persevere until finding a path that works. My sister-in-law Erin gets me as an introvert who needs some quiet time, and cheers me on selflessly. Karen and Terry were always the first to step up as practical helpers with our sons when I needed time for practicing therapy, writing, or going out and having fun. All of these people were an important part of the creation of this book, and I am counting on them all to continue being incredible so I can keep doing what I love.

Most of all, I thank God for giving me the desire and opportunity to write and guiding my steps to this point of joy and celebration in my journey.

INTRODUCTION

Week after week, the preacher carefully and intentionally heaved the enormous book onto the lectern. He flipped it open and read words that sounded odd to me. The Bible heroes' dialect and conversations were different from the conversations I heard, even between church members, in my small Midwestern town. A man got swallowed by a huge fish and spent three days in its belly? The whole world flooded, and only one family survived? Eat my body and drink my blood? It was all a bit confusing to my concrete-operational, elementary-school-aged mind. Still, hundreds gathered week after week at our church, and every church in town, with reverence to the One who we were told authored the Bible's words. The church's reminder that I needed some help with life resonated with me, and I was open to getting help wherever help could be found. Still, there was something compelling to me about God and the Bible, and I wanted more of it.

I have brought many parts of myself to the Bible over time. As a child, I brought the part of me hungry to learn and hear stories of faith amid struggle. Noah survived the flood, Moses survived the wilderness, and Jesus survived the cross. I could survive hard things too. I sensed that there was something spiritually important about the Bible's stories and their characters. I was taught to be brave like Esther, persistent and receptive like Noah, uncompromising like Daniel, and committed to the Ten Commandments like Moses.

At some point in my childhood I began to approach the Bible like I approached God and other people; I asked what it expected of me. I readily questioned my own desires and preferences and looked for a concrete guide for what was right and good. I looked outwardly for wisdom with the hope that it would show up in my parents, friends, and church. When I approached the Bible, I found a script and a role to play: rules and expectations with which I could do my best to comply. However, the Bible's size, density, and peculiar language intimidated me. The columns of tiny words often left me with more questions than answers. It felt like a tall order to understand, much less follow, all the Bible's demands. When I noticed desires within myself that seemed incompatible with the Bible's teachings, I cast them aside with a dismissive sort of shame. My well-behaved, studious self was welcome at church, while more expressive parts of myself felt restricted by others' rules, including the Bible's.

By high school, I'd been confirmed in the church and knew more about God and the significance of religious practices like baptism and Communion. I prayed, but mostly I experienced God as a cosmic parent whom I needed to please. The expressive parts of me still struggled with church and the Bible, so I searched for and immersed myself in various expressive outlets. When I couldn't put words to how I felt, I could sing about it in an *a cappella* group, play it on the piano, or act it out through becoming a character in a play. Eventually, I was intoxicated by the excitement of independent choices and risks. I rejected and challenged the rule-driven, well-behaved persona I'd developed during my elementary and middle school years. I faced the frustration of falling short of the standard I'd internalized of what it meant to be a good Christian. I tested limits and learned the pleasurable benefits and painful consequences of sinful choices. My view of my actions as sinful led me down a path of shame that felt hard to dispel. My shifting identity caused tension in my faith. I felt more in need of God's love than ever and, at the same time, like a moral and spiritual disappointment on every front.

At that point, the Bible's relevance to my life seemed limited. Its guidance proved largely useless in the face of teenage dating relationships, a declining body image, and a persistent cloud of uncertainty and self-doubt regarding the future. I felt betrayed by my faith; it did not seem to offer much in the face of present, relevant struggles in my day-to-day life. For a brief time, I became convinced that God could not exist.

During college, I became fascinated by what motivated people, by what motivated me. The expressive parts of myself found a home in the field of psychology. As I became skilled at naming my emotional strengths and struggles, I took them to the Bible, looking expectantly for guidance. I turned to campus groups that offered an emotional expression of Christianity. I carried my tattered New Living Translation in my backpack most places I went and read it often. I served two summers at a Christian camp for at-risk youth, sang praise songs, and used the word *saved* a lot. This type of spirituality had an emotional flavor to it, which I needed, loved, and consumed. The reality of Jesus loving me and inhabiting my heart brought renewed mystery and warmth to my understanding of spirituality. It felt pleasantly incompatible with the lists of rules I mentally compiled that would keep everyone around me happy. This mystery and warmth would become the most enduring aspect of my faith.

At camp, I met Dusty. After dating for three short months, Dusty proposed to me, and we were married the following year. In marriage, I brought my desire for intimacy to the Bible. I saw the ways that even the best marriages are limited, that no spouse can fulfill all of our longings. I wanted a person who could meet all my needs, and I wanted to be a person who could meet all of another's needs. Neither is a possibility. I experienced an intimate connection to God through the Bible that transcended the limits of even my best human connections.

During the early years of our marriage, Dusty and I attended Presbyterian, Episcopal, Missionary Alliance, Baptist, Vineyard, Independent/Evangelical Mega, and Methodist churches. One church we attended for five years had thousands of members, professional musicians, and weekly parking issues. Another, where Dusty served as an interim pastor, stood among the farms of rural Indiana and averaged about twenty-five people on any given Sunday. The Bible was the common denominator in all those places, though the people and their interpretations of it varied greatly.

Over six years of graduate study, I became well versed in the language of emotion, cognition, and behavior. I was in my element in academia. I thrived and felt valued. The Bible held a sustaining presence in my life but I admittedly looked at it like a misunderstood friend whom I was unsure how to support. I still loved it and it still spoke to me, but it was not highly regarded among some of my colleagues in psychology. For them, the Bible and its adherents represent the essence of racism and bigotry and a lack of cultural awareness. I embraced my Christian identity *and* the challenge to be a culturally sensitive Christian.

After finishing my degree, I provided individual and group therapy at an intensive treatment center for people with eating disorders. It was intense and emotionally demanding work. I had a strong spiritual foundation, but I still needed good therapy to face my resurfacing self-doubt and lack of self-worth. A great therapist helped me through the early life of my three sons, one miscarriage, some marital bumps, and the untimely deaths of several friends. I emerged from therapy a more grounded person, able to embrace my strengths, acknowledge my struggles, and ask for help when I need it.

Throughout graduate school and the early years of my career, the magnetic pull and emotional highs of evangelical Christianity faded in their appeal. I wondered if I was losing my faith when we left our popular mega-church in Atlanta, but I was drawn to a quieter, more contemplative expression of Christianity. My faith grew stronger as I spent time meditating on scripture and listening to God in prayer. I gravitated toward more academic theological readings and discussions, and I further explored the connections between psychology and spirituality. One without the other seemed to be lacking something important. After solid progress in my personal therapy, I could approach my faith from a healthier place.

Now, as a parent, I have begun to revisit faith from a child's perspective, to discuss faith in the context of a preschooler's worldview. We were drawn to our current church by its strong preschool program. Our church's theology strikes a healthy balance between acknowledging our need for God and embracing our infinite worth as creatures made in the complex and creative image of God. When I embrace both sides of that dichotomy, I discover that I am free to live in faith in unrestricted ways. I can move forward in the humility of needing God while I stand strong in the belief that I reflect and embody valuable aspects of God.

From life as a young child through life with my own young children, the Bible has revealed new and enlightening perspectives to me. Over time, the Bible has become a sort of healthy parental presence in my life; it provides some clear direction and generates some frustration. As any good parent does, the Bible remains stable and tolerates my frustration rather than intrusively trying to fix it. Though other people have imposed their interpretations of the Bible on me, the Bible hasn't imposed itself. The Bible's familiar, comforting passages are there for me anytime I choose to go to them. The Bible remains steady, stable, and readily available. It does not remove itself from me when I repeatedly violate its codes but rather remains ever-present and urges me to be still. Its passages provide a quiet nudge that reminds me that the Lord leads me and restores my soul. (See Psalm 23.) Sometimes, it speaks to me in bolder ways, less like a nudge and more like a confrontation or intervention from a beloved friend. It shows me the parts of myself I like least while simultaneously guarding, preserving, and defending my worth. The Bible allows me to come to it on my own terms. When I am ready, it lies open with unguarded honesty and always seems to reveal what I most need to read.

My theological training is limited to my own reading of Bible commentaries and writings of theologians, a couple of undergraduate courses, and one seminary course. The bulk of my expertise lies in my study of psychology and my experience of providing group and individual therapy to clients. I know people and the dynamics between people very well, and I see them in the stories of the Bible. I can read people and recognize the unspoken as well as the spoken content of peoples' lives and relationships. As a therapist, I've spent the last eighteen years talking openly and listening to all kinds of stories and feelings.

I've learned that people flourish when we feel seen and participate more actively and authentically in relationships. I've learned to notice and receive more love from others. As a result, I've been able to take in more uplifting and relevant messages from the Bible too. I can approach prayer with radical acceptance of myself. I can let the working out of my salvation be a work in progress.

When my youngest son, Zach, was a baby, I signed up for a Disciple Bible study in our United Methodist Church. In one year, I read 70 percent of the Bible and digested it with a small group of people from church. We spent two hours per week meeting together to study and reflect. I wrote more, gave sermons at a small Wednesday night service, and asked a lot of questions. I began to experience the Bible differently. More than ever before I recognized that Bible stories have symbolic meanings, and they jumped out at me. The nuanced feelings I saw in the characters felt especially and immediately relevant to my life. All aspects of my life are intimately touched by faith, and I discovered that the stories of the Bible transport ancient truths into modern and deeply personal relevance. The Bible doesn't just teach us about Noah, Moses, Jesus, and Mary. It teaches us about ourselves.

The Bible offers a way for us to come to Jesus, to understand who he was, what he did, and what he still offers to us today. In the Gospel of John, Jesus speaks to a crowd and offers an invitation to come to him, to believe in him, and to drink living water. (See John 7:37-38.) Beyond offering the basic tenets of the Christian faith, the Bible is a living document that sustains us today. As I read the Bible, it seems to come alive; it engages me and reveals things about me. I cannot predict or control when it will happen, but if I consistently approach its words with an open heart, something spiritually interactive occurs. Through its words and stories, the Bible can speak to and stir the most vulnerable, unspoken corners of my experience. Despite its apparent inconsistencies and puzzling language, it reveals sustenance and support. Through its characters, it reveals struggle and feels more like something I want to read, something I relate to, something like me. I now experience the Bible as something beyond a script or symbol of faith; it truly serves as a source of life and sustenance.

When no one around me seems to get it, the Bible reveals what will bring me life. The Bible remains the same when we are sitting on our most stagnant, uninteresting plateau of hopelessness, depleted and spiritually dehydrated as well as when we are on our invincible peaks, full of life, ready to take on all the challenges ahead. It steadies our uncertainty, tempers our impulsivity, and pushes us beyond our cozy corner chair of passivity. As we open up the Bible and open up ourselves, our spiritual encounter with the text leads to change.

How to Use This Study

At the end of the day, I embrace Dusty and my three sons; my dog, Furter, curls up next to me. As my mind reviews the events of the day and prepares itself for tomorrow, I wonder whether what I am building, my family and work, will stand when storms come. Suddenly, I become Noah working on his ark, hammering in earnest and anticipating the impending waters while skeptical observers offer nothing but negativity. Noah doesn't just build an ark. Noah invests in something that seems foolish and like a waste of time to his observers. He builds something enormous and receives step-by-step instructions from God on how to do it. He weathers the worst storm the world has seen, huddled together with his immediate family and some animals. Aren't we all drawn to dreams of doing that same thing on some level? In Noah's story I learn to keep hammering and building, to trust God's next step, to look for and cling to my allies. I can be sure that life will bring floods, and I am equally convinced that I will want to have built something meaningful when it does. Noah's Ark is no longer a story that seems far-removed and unlikely. It's a story about me.

Maybe you've approached the Bible like I used to as a set of expectations, an antiquated work of literature, or a book of ancient stories, far-removed from this century. I invite you to use this study to open yourself to the possibility that the Bible has something to say to you on a personal level, something that is relevant to your modern life. Let's approach these stories together with an open mind. Do not feel compelled to make significant spiritual decisions. Instead, listen deeply to the stories of faith, and be willing to find yourself in them.

In this book I will recount some of what the Bible has revealed to me about myself, and I hope that each story will speak to you as well. Each story in this book has taught me something about myself, immediately relevant and deeply personal. Each lesson challenged me, prompted me to visit the less comfortable corners of my psyche, and showed me what needed my attention. The truths contained in these stories have relevance for you too. Maybe you will hear the same message God spoke to me, or maybe what you learn will be entirely different. If you read with an open heart and mind, I believe the personal truths you need to hear will be revealed.

Each of the six sections of this book explores one of the following ways the Bible can teach you about yourself: what you already have, what to do with your pain, where you can find truth, how your relationships heal, why your faith needs fun, and what is next for you.

Approach the Bible as a friend who wants to give you a gift with no strings attached, a gift that shows that your friend really gets you, really knows your pain, and really loves you. Come to the Bible with healthy doses of critical thinking and respect for what its stories can teach you. Come ready to receive self-awareness. If you've ever looked at the Bible as a list of rules, an unreasonable, outdated, patriarchal document, or a collection of fictional stories, that is fine. Try to read it one more time with the expectation that it may also teach you something about yourself.

The format of this book lends itself to individual study over six weeks. Each week offers five reflections and a weekend practice that integrates the concepts of the week and suggests an activity to put into practice the ideas you've read about. I recommend completing one reading per day Monday through Friday and trying the weekend practice on Saturday or Sunday.

The book also lends itself to a group study over a suggested period of seven or eight weeks. If reading with a group, you may adjust the days you complete each reading based on the day your group meets. For example, members of a Wednesday night book club group might read the daily reflections Thursday through Monday and complete the Weekend Practice Tuesday or Wednesday in preparation for group discussion at Wednesday night's meeting. In a seven- or eight-week format, the first meeting can focus on setting a tone and expectations and discussing the introduction. You can then discuss one section a week for the next six meetings. You may choose to spend an eighth week doing something social to mark the completion of your time together as a group and tie up any last topics of discussion. Please note that there is a **Facilitator's Guide** at the end of the book, which offers a structured way to review and discuss what you've read.

Even if you are reading this book individually, you may find some of the content in the Facilitator's Guide helpful for personal reflection.

In preparation for your journey through this book, begin with the following introductory practice. Move on to that practice now to prepare for what the Bible will reveal to you about yourself.

Introductory Practice

Begin by writing down in this book, in a journal, or on a note card three questions you have about yourself. They do not have to be spiritual or psychological in nature, but they can be. They should be important questions, things that you feel have real significance for how your life will take shape going forward. These questions should be personal enough that you would feel greater clarity and purpose and a sense of relief if you had some insight into these questions. If you're struggling to come up with some, consider some of the following examples. They may be relevant to you or lead you to your own questions: *How can I feel calmer and more focused day to day? How can I stop feeling so down and self-critical? How can I have a healthier relationship with food and my body? How can I work through the conflict in a particular relationship in my life? How can I feel more direction and purpose in my work? How can I make better decisions as a parent?*

Your task in this practice is immediate and ongoing: Today pray a short, simple prayer asking God to reveal at least part of an answer to your questions as you read this book and the Bible stories I reference. As you read and sense what God is revealing to you, open your mind to hearing the Bible's stories in a way relevant to your life. The truths revealed to you through biblical characters or even through my interaction with the Bible stories may provide some valuable insights into the questions you are asking about yourself today. The following questions will help you reflect on each Bible story:

1. **How do I see myself in this story?** Which character represents you? Could different characters represent different parts of you? How does this story help you relate to God?

2. **What is this story teaching me about myself?** Is it highlighting a personality characteristic that you need to address? Is it bringing to mind a relationship fraught with unresolved conflict or a need for greater love? Is the story nudging you to set a boundary in a relationship because you see it heading in a direction that is not good for you?

3. **So what?** In graduate school, one of my professors asked us to approach research data, analysis, and results with the question, "So what?" We can get lost in the details, and this question helps filter our reading through a lens of critical thinking that pulls forth relevant information about what matters most in applying the greater conclusions. I think we benefit in approaching the Bible in the same way. Noah built an ark. So what? How does this make a difference in my day-to-day life? How does this story change things for me in a meaningful way?

There are truths in the stories of the Bible that can directly impact and improve your psychological health. When you bring your whole self with all your questions, doubts, and beliefs to these ancient stories, the Bible can teach you about yourself.

WEEK ONE: WHAT YOU ALREADY HAVE

Come Down

When Jesus reached the spot, he looked up and said to him, "Zacchaeus, come down immediately. I must stay at your house today."
—Luke 19:5 (NIV)

One summer I worked at an adventure camp in a rural town outside the city of Timişoara, Romania. My friend and I helped college students speak conversational English between hikes and other outings. One day, our climb was rocky and jagged, and there had been some snake sightings earlier that day. We were a long hike away from roads or vehicles, much less a hospital or town. The leaders of our group stood at the top of the mountain and created a makeshift rappelling wall out of a cliff that stood high above the tree line. I was less adventurous than my friend and opted to watch the rappelling from below. She ascended the hill and rappelled down the side of the mountain without hesitation. With some urging on her part, I decided to try it. The climb up the side of the mountain was difficult, but I was used to long, difficult climbs. The scariest part was coming down. For me to rappel safely and effectively down the mountain, I had to lean back and trust that the rope would hold me. With my feet propped flat against the cliff as I lowered myself into the harness, I looked over my shoulder and my stomach did a little flip. I settled into my harness and began my descent. I saw the treetops and the small figures of the people below, and I tried not to envision the rope coming loose or snapping. I prayed that God would keep me safe. Once I relaxed into the descent, I felt the fear give way to a thrilling rush of adrenaline. I felt strong and empowered.

We find the story of Zacchaeus, a tax collector, in the book of Luke. Luke, a physician and advocate for the marginalized, has a unique way of presenting the compassion Jesus has for those who have been shunned by others.[1] Jesus honors those who seek him out despite whatever they have done, whatever they have become in life. Zacchaeus has accumulated vast wealth through dishonest and manipulative practices as a tax collector. But Zacchaeus seeks Jesus with urgency, which suggests that he seeks something more than the wealth he has attained. Blocked by the crowd, he climbs up a tree to get a better view. He wants to see who Jesus is from his own vantage point. He ascends into the tree isolated from the crowd. He elevates himself above everyone, including Jesus.

Jesus has a life-changing encounter in mind for Zacchaeus, one that Zacchaeus cannot have predicted or orchestrated. Zacchaeus does not have to climb the tree for Jesus to know he is there. Jesus sees us even when we cannot or do not want to see him. Even though Zacchaeus is judged and discounted by his community, Jesus joyfully receives him. As the father runs to the prodigal son in Luke 15:11-32 and the shepherd goes after the lost sheep in Luke 15:1-7, Jesus seeks out Zacchaeus.

Aren't there times when all of us climb in search of a better position or perspective? Whether in the world of academics, athletics, personal finances, or appearance, we believe that we can somehow gain a better vantage point. Even in our perspective of Jesus, many of us are more comfortable observing Jesus from a distance than participating in the more intimate experience he has in mind. Sometimes our climb becomes tiring, especially when we accumulate unrealistic self-standards for what it means to be a Christian. We take on more volunteer positions, help more people, and attend more meetings. We begin to equate Christianity with moral perfection, and we experience waves of shame when we inevitably fall short of our standards.

Fortunately, Jesus does not thrust upon us the expectations that we place upon ourselves. Instead, he honors those who seek him out. He calls us to remain in him, as he remains in us. The call of Jesus is first and foremost a relational call. Jesus' initial, direct command to Zacchaeus is not that he reform his life, not that he be a little nicer, not that he make amends with the people he has cheated. Jesus urges Zacchaeus only to come down and engage with him. He extends a loving invitation and investment. Jesus asks that Zacchaeus show up when Jesus shows up in the comfort and vulnerability of his own living room.

When we approach Jesus as an historical figure, a vague entity, or an image on stained glass, our relationship with him can become one that occurs on our own terms. We feel as though we can choose when, how long, and the depth to which he can take part in our lives. But when we invite him into our car ride home from church, into our living rooms, and into our messy lives, we invite a different experience altogether.

Our homes reflect the truth about our lives. The neatness or disarray, the decor, the colors, and the degree of comfort and warmth represent our experiences. Our homes reflect a set of values, personality, and a general attitude toward life. At this stage of my life, the superheroes and Legos scattered on the floor say, "We have three little boys." The mountain of unfolded laundry says, "There just doesn't seem to be enough time." But I hope the overall feel says, "Come in and be comfortable. We have kids, and we have fun together. You are welcome to be here without having to be organized, neat, and presentable." I intentionally refrain from hurriedly cleaning everything to perfection every time someone comes over, mainly because I don't have the energy, but also because it communicates that my house is not always clean, and that is the truth. Jesus sees the truth that lies beyond our walls and illusions of perfection. When we welcome Jesus into our everyday lives, we open ourselves up to be changed and transformed. We no longer need to be isolated or dependent on our own pursuits.

When Jesus calls, Zacchaeus does not contemplate the pros and cons. He does not do a cost-benefit analysis and talk with a therapist about the potential emotional growth that might occur should he come down from the tree. In the core of his being, and with no real ambivalence, he knows the only choice that he can make. It is the same choice the disciples make when they drop their fishing nets. It is immediate, and it is personal. Though the crowd grumbles and judges him as a sinner, Zacchaeus hurries down from the tree and joyfully welcomes Jesus. He doesn't seem worried about the state of his house, and I can imagine that Jesus didn't spend time attending to Zacchaeus's material home so much as his spiritual one. Are we in such an admirable hurry to come down from reliance on our own resources, our own comfortable, distanced view of Jesus to an uncertain encounter amid our messes?

I get the sense that the specific changes Zacchaeus promises to make are not out of dutiful obligation but joyfully prompted by his encounter with Jesus. According to the law, Zacchaeus only has to add a fifth of what he's wrongfully taken from others, but he far exceeds that by restoring it fourfold. Having taken advantage of everyone in his path, Zacchaeus is an unlikely candidate for generosity and restitution, yet that is exactly what occurs. In my experience of Jesus, the connection with him prompts us to radical, uncomfortable, and unexpected actions. The more closeness I experience with Jesus, the more I want to hurry to come down and be with him. Ironically, when I can let go of my striving, that is when I open myself, as Zacchaeus did, to true change. What do you need to let go of, leave behind, or do to come closer to Jesus? Maybe it is setting aside ten quiet minutes a day to listen for his voice. Maybe it involves an honest and uncensored prayer.

After making my decision to try rappelling, I came down from the mountain. My decision to come down was the tough part. But the descent filled me with a rush of excitement and awe. When Jesus calls to you, are you willing to come down? Risk an encounter with Jesus that may turn out to be more than you expected. Allow your life to be more about connection than achievement.

Wherever you find yourself in this story, it is my hope that you will meet Jesus there and allow his presence to visit you without feeling compelled to tidy up first or display your achievements. I hope you will walk away from your visit with Jesus feeling loved and sought after by the One who seeks after all humanity.

Read Luke 19:1-10. Ask yourself three questions: How do I see myself in this story? What is this story teaching me about myself? So what?

I Cannot Walk with These

David strapped Saul's sword over the armor, and he tried in vain to walk, for he was not used to them. Then David said to Saul, "I cannot walk with these; for I am not used to them." So David removed them.

—1 Samuel 17:39

When I was in preschool, I wished I could bring home all the stuffed animals that sat on the shelf of a toy store. They were stuffed into a line, and I thought they looked sad. I wanted to help them and take care of them. They had such a boring existence just watching everyone else going about their lives but not being able to participate in any of it. In some sense, I was feeling sadness about my own passivity and about my own fear to really engage with people or in activities I might enjoy. I carefully observed, admired, and befriended people with very strong preferences. I felt drawn to their sense of certainty about what they wanted. As a quiet and reserved child, I observed and guessed what my teachers, parents, and coaches expected from me. I sought to keep the peace, even if that meant compromising my preferences in situations with friends and family members. I adopted an attitude of self-doubt and assumed other people knew better how to approach and solve problems. I got used to a very passive role and convinced myself that it was okay because I was accepted. But many of those relationships did not encourage me to live in a way that was true to the complex and unique person God created me to be.

19

When I was a child, I attended a Lutheran Church a block away from my house in rural Illinois. I first heard the story of David and Goliath around the same time I wished to bring home all the stuffed animals from the toy store. I remember admiring David, the unlikely young hero, and feeling intimidated by the giant Goliath. David still inspires me, and Goliath still intimidates me. David's dilemma in the face of Goliath illustrates a tension in the Christian faith. On the one hand, we are dependent on God and cannot do anything apart from Jesus. (See John 15:5.) On the other hand, we are capable of doing even greater works than those Jesus performed. (See John 14:12.) Sometimes the challenge of faith is to hold two truths at once and to sit with the complexity and tension. Remembering we are not self-sufficient keeps us from pride and self-idealization. Remembering we are capable empowers us when we might feel immobilized. We need Jesus, *and* through Jesus we are capable of anything.

The giant Goliath is the obvious enemy in the story. He intimidates everyone and scares an entire army of people. But Saul's voice presents some challenges too. Saul makes two counterproductive statements to David. Fortunately, David has a wise response for both of them.

"You are not able," says Saul (1 Sam. 17:33). Saul wrongly assumes that David is not capable of conquering Goliath. It is an understandable assumption given the obvious difference in physical size between David and Goliath. But Saul's estimate of David and his comparison between David and Goliath are based on his limited knowledge and immediate perception. Our initial perceptions of visual realities do not constitute the whole truth about any person. We can inadvertently send Saul's disempowering message when we compare people according to our first impressions. We fail to consider the power of faith and the value of past experience. Another's faith can surpass our expectations. Another's experience can surpass our expectations too.

David responds wisely by stating the truth about his faith in God and the truth about his experience in similar situations. Instead of caving to doubt, David reminds Saul that he single-handedly strikes down lions and bears while keeping his father's sheep. He is a good candidate to face the giant warrior. David also knows the truth about God. His memories of God's provision in the face of lions and bears fuel the faith he needs to face Goliath. David demonstrates faith that he can conquer Goliath. He does not let Saul's condescending estimate define his identity. David's courageous words remind us to own our experiences and to step forward in faith. Too often we allow others to define our worth, our potential, our roles, and our preferences. God's advocacy for us empowers us to embrace challenges with a peace that transcends the understanding of observers.

Next Saul attempts to clothe and protect David with Saul's armor: "He put a bronze helmet on his head and clothed him with a coat of mail. David strapped Saul's sword over the armor, and he tried in vain to walk, for he was not used to them" (1 Sam. 17:38-39). Saul wrongfully assumes that his solution will be David's solution. Saul considers only the lens of his own armor and protection and closes himself off to the possibility that another method of protection and weaponry might be more suitable for David.

During my graduate school training, I sought my own therapy for personal growth. Years later, interventions that had changed my life did not always work for my own clients. Like Saul, we tend to assume that what works for us will work for others. My graduate professors taught me to think like a researcher. Skeptical of anecdotal evidence, they pointed me to bodies of research that were controlled, generalized, and replicated. One dramatic success story does not guarantee the same experience for others. People live out their faith in different ways. Even when bodies of research point toward one solution, outliers remain.

David is an outlier. While the Israelites need armor, David needs five stones, a slingshot, and his faith in God. David's second wise response is, "I cannot walk with these" (1 Sam. 17:39). David knows himself well enough to know that Saul's armor is not his best defense. He trusts an internal prompting of the Spirit and his own self-knowledge above what appears to be the best strategy according to the experts around him. He removes the armor, and in doing so, he removes the burden of what others think he needs. David instead relies on what he knows will allow him to prevail over Goliath. Though it appears foolish to observers, his faith in God and reliance on his own experience allow him to experience a victory that will benefit his people. David picks up five stones from a dried riverbed. David's greatest defense is right in front of him in the form of common, everyday items rather than the impressive and extravagant armor that Saul offers him. Consider that what you need may be right in front of you. We do not necessarily need something extraordinary or impressive to do mighty work for God.

Over the years, I have learned to trust myself more. I know now that it is okay to disagree and enter into conflict with the strong personalities of the world, as long as I stay connected to the truth about God and my experiences. When others challenge me, I find security in God's love and full acceptance of me. Whether or not others acknowledge my training and life experiences, I know they are valid. I was there. I have learned that when powerful people suggest armor, sometimes I need to decline. Sometimes, I need stones.

Instead of thrusting doubt and armor toward David, Saul could help David choose the five stones. Saul could trust and empower David as a voice of silent support. Instead of imposing our own wisdom, we would be wise to look for the five stones others already carry with them. If we listen to others' experiences and empower them to take steps of faith based on their experience, we may see that they already have the resources that lead to victory over the challenges in their lives. Consider the unwanted armor you use in your attempts to clothe and equip those around you. A type of protection you insist upon may actually weigh down someone else. Instead of determining who is qualified for God's work based on limited perceptions, take the time to suspend your judgment and listen for others' wisdom about their potential and their role in God's work.

We can embrace David's wisdom when we hear others saying, "You are not able." We can speak the truth about our experiences and about what God has done for us. When others try to clothe you with their armor, consider that God may be showing you a different path. Others' methods may not be a good fit for you and may weigh you down. Speak the truth, and remove the burden of armor that doesn't fit. As well-intentioned as it may be, armor you're not used to carrying may do more harm than good. Allow God to work through you in unexpected ways. Trust that God will show you the ways in which you are able to face and conquer Goliath. Pick up the stones.

Read 1 Samuel 17:19-49. Ask yourself three questions: How do I see myself in this story? What is this story teaching me about myself? So what?

Your Own Good Samaritan

He went to him and bandaged his wounds, having poured oil and wine on them. Then he put him on his own animal, brought him to an inn, and took care of him.

—Luke 10:34

After a night out with a group of friends in the spring of my first year in college, we stumbled into our respective dorm hallways during the early morning hours. I had fun that night, but a nagging feeling of emptiness and struggle lingered beneath the surface. I made my way down the dorm's corridor and had almost reached my door when I saw a neighbor, a friend. She knew me well enough to sense that I'd been feeling down. She invited me to hang out in her room, and she made me a bowl of soup. I remember her simple act of kindness with gratitude today, over twenty years later. I got the sense that I was truly welcome and could stay as long as I wanted to stay. We exchanged stories about high school and our families and friends. She treated me with respect, with no hint of condescension or pity.

Throughout the latter part of high school and into my first year of college, I'd been stuck in an emotional ditch. Past relationships and lingering memories hung over my head like a dark cloud. But I didn't have to explain that to my neighbor that night. She did not extend judgment. Instead, she offered hospitality and a listening ear. We laughed a lot. She let me know she was there for me. Sometimes my internal emotional storms felt like too much, and I just wanted to escape from their isolating burden. But her kindness gave me a renewed confidence that I would be okay. Amid my emotional pain, she paused and addressed me instead of ignoring, judging, or walking by me. I was the wounded traveler on the roadside; she was my good Samaritan.

The Gospel of Luke records Jesus' parable of the good Samaritan. (See Luke 10:25-37.) A wounded traveler lies beaten and near death on the side of a road that leads from Jerusalem to Jericho, a notoriously dangerous path that drops 3,600 feet over a mere twenty miles. The jagged, rocky passages make robberies and injuries commonplace. Forging the road alone involves a high risk of danger or injury.[1] Several passersby see the wounded man on the roadside and respond in various ways. A priest looks, crosses the road, and passes on the other side. A Levite also notes the presence of the wounded man but keeps walking. Then, a Samaritan approaches the man. He stops and lovingly attends to the wounded traveler. He extends mercy and practical, nurturing assistance.

The Samaritan never questions the traveler about how he has ended up on the roadside. There are no conditions to his aid. He lifts the traveler onto his donkey and takes him to an inn. The Samaritan finds food and shelter for the traveler. He pays for the stranger's immediate and short-term needs. The Samaritan must be a trusted man. After all, the innkeeper takes on the care of the traveler and believes the Samaritan's promise to return and pay in full for the stranger's care.

Through this story, Jesus calls us to respond to those in need, and I believe that includes responding to our own needs. We need to be good Samaritans to ourselves as well as to others by extending self-compassion every day in small, practical ways. For instance, people with eating disorders rarely need to be told to be more compassionate toward other people. They are often some of the most caring, sensitive, and nurturing people we know. They are the ones who put everyone else's needs before their own and who are willing to sacrifice their own comfort and preferences. Often they have easy temperaments and excel in school and in extracurricular pursuits. But too often, wounded travelers with a lack of self-compassion lie beneath the surface of all the generosity and achievement. These travelers need to be nurtured back to health by accepting permission to eat, to ask for help, and to honor their bodies, voices, and preferences. Likewise, we need to locate within ourselves the Samaritan to the self, the part of us that is willing to address pain rather than look away from it. What choice will we make as we see a glimpse of our suffering self on the side of the road?

The characters in the good Samaritan story can represent the complexity of our internal states. Psychologists like Sigmund Freud and Eric Berne have established that we are complex beings with multiple internal states and systems that interact with one another.[2,3] Think about times when you feel more childlike, times when you feel more like a rebellious adolescent, or times when you feel like a wise caretaker. We carry these multiple selves with us, and they respond to one another internally as we work out our spirituality in light of our past, present, and future. We can view the characters in the parable of the good Samaritan as a collection of internal selves who react in different ways when they witness our emotional pain.

The Levite and the priest represent the parts of ourselves that overlook our emotional pain. We recognize it, but we are unwilling to deal with it. Perhaps we are distracted by our other responsibilities in life. Perhaps we think something else is more important. Those hearing Jesus tell this parable would have expected the next character in the story to be an Israelite without the duties of a priest or Levite; they would have expected the one who helps to be someone like them. But instead, it is a Samaritan—an enemy to the hearers and a stranger to the wounded—who provides the help to the traveler.

We can respond to our pain with the Samaritan part of ourselves, a part that unexpectedly exceeds expectations and comes to our own aid. Our past experiences and current struggles may make it difficult, but we are capable of showing up to care for ourselves. Jesus points to the one who is least likely to extend mercy as the example of showing mercy. Sometimes we feel like the least likely candidates to help ourselves, unequipped and overwhelmed. But locating compassion for ourselves within ourselves can carry us a long way toward healing.

The Samaritan pauses to bandage the wounded man and takes the risk of being attacked by the bandits who attacked the traveler. The Samaritan self makes time to acknowledge pain and to carry pain to where it can find healing and support. The Samaritan also does not take on the whole burden of providing healing. Rather, he gets support from an innkeeper and continues to provide the support he can until the traveler is healed.

We may need to heave an unexpected, deadened part of ourselves onto our donkey and carry it to a place where it can rest and find healing. We may decide, bravely, to face the full weight and mess of our injuries. When we feel the pull of our internal Levite and priest to ignore our pain, we can locate our internal Samaritan. Some resist this. When we work to alleviate our own suffering, it can feel like a self-absorbed experience. However, increasing insight about ourselves can better enable us, in the long run, to meet the needs of others. Once we understand our internal dynamics and motivations, we need not fear them, and we are free to use more of our energy to focus on others.

I was the wounded traveler in my own story, and I needed to locate a Samaritan within myself. I had left by the wayside some of my complex and uncomfortable feelings. Something may happen in your life that brings to light a part of you that is suffering. You will see it there on the side of the road, in need of help. You will have a choice. You will benefit from pausing in your journey to address visible or invisible wounds that immobilize you, that keep you stuck on the wayside. You may, like the Samaritan, extend mercy and compassion. You may need to pay the innkeeper for some help, as the Samaritan did. Maybe your payment will be to a therapist, a trainer, a coach, or a mentor. The Samaritan offers a deposit with an open-ended promise to pay for whatever it costs to restore the wounded to health. Consider a temporary adjustment in your life, whether financial or of your time, and pay what you can afford for emotional support.

Just as neither the Levite nor the priest needs to rush by the wounded traveler, we do not need to ignore our own emotional or physical pain. Rather, we can stop and acknowledge our suffering and ask for help in restoring the wounded parts of ourselves to life. We can respond to our wounds with mercy. Be a good Samaritan to yourself.

Read Luke 10:25-37. Ask yourself three questions: How do I see myself in this story? What is this story teaching me about myself? So what?

Mirror, Mirror

Now we see only a reflection as in a mirror; then we shall see face to face. Now I know in part; then I shall know fully, even as I am fully known.

—1 Corinthians 13:12 (NIV)

My clients with eating disorders often struggle with mirrors, which can become a source of obsession, a tool for self-criticism, and a harbinger of shame, as their disease drives them to seek a sense of control. As my clients recover from their eating disorders, the mirror holds less power. They learn to experience control in other ways and to let go of that which is not in their control. One of the hallmarks of a healthy body image is the ability to acknowledge what is in our control versus out of our control when it comes to our bodies.[1] For instance, we all have a set point weight where our individual bodies want to settle, where we function best. That set point may or may not fall where we want it to fall, or where our culture tells us it should fall. The set point weight varies from person to person. Because of individual genetic differences, any one of us can do only so much to alter our weight. There is a range that makes sense and works for each individual body. We are a diverse species, created in all colors, shapes, and sizes.

Mirrors give us some feedback about our bodies. We can recognize changes in height and weight. A mirror's reflection can help us choose clothing that flatters our body shape in colors that suit our complexions and hairstyles that fit our personality and self-identity. We can observe our expressions and the physical results of joy, sadness, and fatigue. Mirrors can help us make some adjustments. When the mirror tells me there's something in my teeth, I remove it. If my hair is sticking up in a way I did not intend, I straighten it. On the other hand, when I get a clothing style just right or like the way my hair looks, I take note and seek to replicate what led me to have these positive experiences. Yet certain factors, like genetic tendencies, are out of my control. My straight hair simply would not accept the perms of the eighties. I have a particular height and set point weight. My fair skin requires a lot of sunscreen and tends to burn rather than tan, and I have a family history of skin cancer. I have blond hair and blue eyes. I accept and seek to embrace these realities.

Mirrors hold an interesting sort of power over us. We make a daily assessment of how we look, what we present to the world at first glance. The mirror can hold too much power at times and cause us to zero in on the aspect of our physical appearance we like the least or cause us to cling to what we feel good about and feel pressure to maintain it. If we spend too much energy trying to change aspects of our bodies that are out of our control, we get frustrated. While mirrors often reflect realities about our appearance, there are many things central to my life that a mirror cannot show me. A mirror cannot reflect my birth experiences or how it felt to hold a newborn baby. It cannot tell me what it was like to be up at all hours feeding and rocking those babies. It cannot give me any feedback about the best strategies for raising children or advise me how best to balance my life. It cannot tell me anything about whom or what I love. It cannot tell me what I want, what I need, or what to prioritize. It's an incomplete picture. We would be wise not to let an incomplete picture take over the whole picture.

Two passages in the Bible involve discussion of a mirror. One seems to suggest that it is not good to assess ourselves in the mirror and then forget what we've seen there: "If any are hearers of the word and not doers, they are like those who look at themselves in a mirror; for they look at themselves and, on going away, immediately forget what they were like" (James 1:23-24). Sometimes we do not look in the mirror often enough. One day I led a ninety-minute therapy group only to go to the bathroom afterward and see that I had a small piece of spinach in my teeth. Another time I ran into a friend in the farmer's market only to realize that the fake tattoos I'd put on my face with my boys the night before were still there in remnants. Too much time away from the mirror can lead to a lack of awareness. When we look in the mirror, we are wise to remember the reflection that we see. In our reflection, we find valuable clues about ourselves. When you look in the mirror, look yourself in the eyes. Do you see joy, gratitude, criticism, emptiness, cloudiness, or clarity? Do you recognize yourself? Do you see energy or fatigue? Are you projecting an image that reveals your personality and identity or one that conceals you? Do you see something different than what others tell you about yourself? What do you believe about yourself as you look at your reflection? Are you consumed with perfecting your appearance, or are you focused on the self-expression of what you want and feel called to present to the world? As you walk away from the mirror, don't forget what you've seen. Tired eyes may signal a need for rest. A new mole may warrant a visit to the dermatologist. Let what you see flow into what you do.

The other passage communicates that what we see in the mirror is deceptively incomplete; whatever is reflected there cannot possibly encompass full knowledge of ourselves: "Now we see only a reflection as in a mirror; then we shall see face to face. Now I know in part; then I shall know fully, even as I am fully known" (1 Cor. 13:12, NIV). The mirror offers us some truth but not the whole picture. Other people look at us and observe more than our physical appearance. They experience us as our personality, our opinions, and our gifts and talents. The mirror is a start, but relationships tell us more.

The Bible functions as a spiritual mirror; it can show us what we present to the world in a spiritual sense. It can help us discern how to better love ourselves and show us where we need to make changes by bringing into focus our behaviors. When we look at our spiritual reflection, we get to know ourselves better. James urges us not to forget what we see in our spiritual mirror but to walk away changed and ready to adjust as needed.

What we know now is a dim and partial knowing of ourselves. Despite years of therapy, great self-knowledge, spiritual gifts inventories, and a vocabulary for every struggle known to humankind, we can only know ourselves in part. But while we sit with a messy and incomplete knowledge of ourselves, God knows us completely. God gives us relationships for additional perspectives. God gives us the Bible as a spiritual mirror for guidance. We can take an honest look in the mirror, take feedback from others, and look for guidance in God's Word. In moments of revelation and in moments of uncertainty, we can come to the Bible with the belief that it will show us truth about ourselves. We can take in the truth of God's love for us and find a balance between what we can know and control versus what we can accept and embrace.

Read 1 Corinthians 13. Ask yourself three questions: How do I see myself in this story? What is this story teaching me about myself? So what?

Unrestricted

The love of God is this, that we obey his commandments. And his commandments are not burdensome, for whatever is born of God conquers the world.

—1 John 5:3

Our church hosts a week of vacation Bible school every summer. One year, I served on a storytelling team. Each day I acted out the part of Moses, a role I embraced with excitement and a sense of humor. I wore a long robe and a head covering with ropes to fasten it in place along with a long, grey beard. I held a tall staff in my hand. In one of the skits, I carried two stone tablets with the Ten Commandments from Mount Sinai to present to the Israelites. The commands of God were written on heavy stone and were weighty in their significance in the lives of the Israelites. I pretended that my replicas were very difficult to carry even though they were made of a lightweight Styrofoam material. The first letter of John asserts that, through our faith in Christ, God's commands are not a heavy burden. Because of Christ's love in us and Christ's sacrifice for us, God's commandments are not difficult to carry. (See 1 John 5:1-5.) They are more like the Styrofoam. The commands that were initially weighty and burdensome now have become light. (See Matthew 11:30.)

Many persons with eating disorders practice rigid food restriction. Those who restrict food intake usually restrict themselves in other ways too. They may restrict how much they share emotionally in relationships. They may restrict money, self-care, or variety in life experiences. Restriction burdens us when we restrict things that aren't meant to be restricted. Our bodies need a variety of foods. When we eat regular, satisfying meals and snacks, we are much less likely to overeat. In eating disorders, restriction is a big problem. I've often written down "restricting" as a negative symptom and sought to help clients alleviate it. But certain types of restriction translate into freedom. God instructs us to restrict some things, and it's for our benefit. Through the Ten Commandments, God urges that we restrict ourselves from lying, from taking what doesn't belong to us, from discontentment, and from putting anyone or anything on a pedestal that stands above God in our hearts. (See Exodus 20:1-20.) God knows that when we restrict harmful things, we find freedom.

One of my common interventions with clients involves exploring how they can move away from merely trying to alleviate a symptom. Instead, I challenge them to add something positive to their lives. Personal growth accelerates when we are striving toward a goal rather than only trying to alleviate a problem. It is difficult for any of us to muster up enough willpower to stop a negative behavior. We will be more successful when we understand the need that the behavior meets, find a healthier way to meet the need, and actively pursue the other behavior. The need itself is usually a valid human need; we have developed harmful ways of trying to meet the need rather than healthy ones.

Fortunately God doesn't only give us restrictions. God also gives us two central goals to strive for: " 'You shall love the Lord your God with all your heart, and with all your soul, and with all your mind, and with all your strength.' The second is this, 'You shall love your neighbor as yourself.' There is no other commandment greater than these" (Mark 12:30-31).

Nutritionist Ralph Carson wrote a book called *The Brain Fix* about what goes on in our brains when we are addicted to a substance like food or drugs.[1] When we consume an addictive substance, dopamine levels in our brain spike rapidly but only temporarily. A different part of the brain is more connected to the experience of lasting happiness. In people with addictions, this area has a shortage of cells. The good news is that we can increase the number of cells in that part of our brain, which can lead to greater and more lasting happiness. In a separate study, researchers asked high school students what they thought would lead to lasting happiness. Their answers included money, intelligence, beauty, and residences. In response, the researchers looked at the brains of people who won the lottery, had extreme makeovers, gained fame on *American Idol*, and moved to Malibu; but no changes occurred in the part of the brain associated with lasting happiness. We can increase the cells in this area of the brain through other, less glamorous means: meditation, compassion, gratitude, altruism, meaningful relationships with someone you can confide in, and purposeful work.[2] In other words, when we restrict excessive activity, we free up time to meditate. When we restrict criticism, we enable ourselves to be more compassionate. When we restrict greed, we increase gratitude. When we restrict selfish ambition, we allow room for altruism. When we restrict isolation, we increase our capacity for meaningful relationships with confidants. When we restrict meaningless repetition, we open up opportunities for purposeful work. Dr. Carson tells us that when these conditions are present we not only feel better while performing these behaviors but also can achieve lasting happiness.

God knows we need those cells that represent lasting happiness and not just a spurt of momentary pleasure that may be difficult to replicate over and over in any lasting way. So when God gives us a list of behaviors to restrict, we may feel that we are missing out on that quick, momentary burst of pleasure. But the truth is that God provides great momentary joy on occasions *and* goes beyond that, calling us to the things that are not burdens but create in us the potential for long-term, lasting happiness.

When we place excessive restrictions upon ourselves, they become burdens. But when we honor God's commands, we strengthen our faith. And as our faith becomes stronger, we feel less burdened and lighter, freer. When we think of the stone tablets, we also can think of the Styrofoam tablets and the lightness and freedom we can experience in our faith in Christ, which frees us from the burden of the law and empowers us to fulfill it.

Read 1 John 5:1-5. Ask yourself three questions: How do I see myself in this story? What is this story teaching me about myself? So what?

WEEKEND PRACTICE

Your Modern Creed

A creed is a statement of belief. Many church congregations read creeds like the Apostles' Creed and Nicene Creed in unison during church liturgy. Your task this weekend is to create a modern creed that contains your general Christian beliefs and has a personal element to it.

Think about your creed as a summary of your beliefs about faith. Typically, a creed states something about your view of concepts like the Trinity, resurrection, eternity, sin, and forgiveness as well as key events that help shape your faith ("Christ died and then rose again"). The following is the Apostles' Creed:

I believe in God the Father Almighty,
maker of heaven and earth;
And in Jesus Christ his only Son our Lord:
who was conceived by the Holy Spirit,
born of the Virgin Mary,
suffered under Pontius Pilate,
was crucified, dead, and buried;*
the third day he rose from the dead;
he ascended into heaven,
and sitteth at the right hand of God the Father Almighty;
from thence he shall come to judge the quick and the dead.
I believe in the Holy Spirit,
the holy catholic** church,
the communion of saints,
the forgiveness of sins,
the resurrection of the body,
and the life everlasting. Amen.

*Traditional use of this creed includes these words: "He descended into hell."
**universal (UMH, no. 881)

Consider the following questions as you explore what you will choose to include in your creed:

1. Where in my life am I more committed to achievement than to following God's will for my life?
2. Where in my life am I striving to meet others' expectations when God's path for me does not meet those expectations?
3. What area of my emotional life have I neglected? How can I give it loving attention?
4. Where do I claim to see things perfectly when in reality I only see and know part of the picture?
5. What rules do I follow that don't seem to have a point? What rules in scripture can I follow that could free me to love and serve God better?

My answers to these types of questions helped me write a creed of my own:

I believe in God, a loving and powerful nurturer, creator and source of life. I believe in Jesus, who knows and lived the human experience and sacrificed himself to bring salvation to the world. I believe in the Holy Spirit, a counselor and guide who shows us truth and prompts us toward what is right and good. I prioritize extending and receiving love in relationships over individual acheivements. I release myself from others' expectations and attend to my emotional needs. I recognize the limits of knowledge and insight, but I value and deal with what I know. I follow rules that honor God and lead to freedom, while I release myself from excessive demands. I strive to love, move, and create in prayerful and mindful reflection.

Write out your creed on a note card or colored piece of paper. Laminate it if you'd like. It is meant only for you, and you should keep it somewhere where you will see and read it often. Try reading your creed every day for the next week. Take note of how it affects your mind-set, emotions, and internal spiritual state throughout the week.

Little Egypts

The LORD said to Moses, "Pharaoh's heart is unyielding; he refuses to let the people go."

—Exodus 7:14 (NIV)

I slipped down the stairs into the basement of the physics building on Miami University's campus during my sophomore year in college. It was evening, and I was out of breath. I made a mental list of everything I'd just eaten, and my anxiety escalated. I had been running as fast as I could away from my dorm, away from my concerned friends, and away from myself. I felt compelled to take action, to somehow restore a physical and emotional balance. I had eaten an amount of food that felt like a transgression, and I felt trapped in my own efforts to settle the score. I had already been to treatment and restored my weight. Many people assumed I was better, though my closest friends certainly had their suspicions when I continued to make excuses during mealtimes or abruptly disappeared after meals. I figured that using the dorm's community bathrooms would rouse more suspicion, so I was looking for a place on campus to hide. Still as sensitive as I had been as a child and as desperate for control as I had been as a teenager, I ran away from my best sources of love and support and further into a trap that would consume way too much of my energy in years to come. I was desperately miserable and alone. I felt compelled to secrecy out of shame and, at the same time, longed for help.

After that night, enough was enough. I decided to call the university's counseling center. The therapist who interviewed me peered over her clipboard as she asked a list of questions that seemed intrusive. I didn't know if I could trust her, but I was at a loss for what else to do. I couldn't bring myself to tell my parents about the new layers of the problem, so I am sure they also assumed I was doing better. In truth, I was on a downward spiral heading for my lowest point yet. I was always pretty good at presenting an acceptable external self, but not so good at tuning into and communicating the truth of my internal experiences. Acutely attuned to others' expectations, I learned to mold and adapt myself to what was required in any given scenario. Always the A student and successful athlete and musician, I appeared to be doing just fine. People could not see my internal torrential storms of shame and confusion. I attempted to control my weight, food, and caloric intake. But more than that, my focus on numbers and quantifiable problems provided a more manageable focus than the amorphous, less controllable feelings and conundrums my life presented. I had so oriented myself to external expectations that I had lost completely my ability to recognize my true feelings and preferences. Internally, I needed some renovation and healing.

I still like to feel a sense of control, and at times I still struggle to locate my internal truth. We all grasp for a greater sense of control over our lives and construct little worlds that we can manage and control in the face of uncertainty. Those "little Egypts" can feel like the truest part of our experience, but they often mask what we most need to identify and confront within ourselves. Moses knows what it means to walk the path of dangerous uncertainty. He is an unlikely leader of thousands, called to challenge the very people he had known as his family after discovering his true identity as an Israelite. God calls Moses to do something he feels unequipped to handle, something that involves great risk. He feels his calling is not a good fit with his age or spiritual gifts.

When Moses is born, his mother is desperate to save him from state-ordered death. She takes matters into her own hands, and Moses comes to be raised as an Egyptian. Later, amid what might have been an identity crisis, Moses kills an Egyptian for beating a Hebrew slave, who he now understands to be one of his own people. When Pharaoh learns of Moses' act, he seeks to kill Moses. Then Moses retreats to a quieter life in the country, gets married, has children, and lives the day-to-day life of a shepherd. For years, Moses completely avoids Pharaoh and his past sin of murder. It isn't until the age of eighty that Moses sees the burning bush, hears the clear voice of God calling to him in the wilderness, and delivers his famous message to Pharaoh: "Let my people go" (Exod. 7:16).

Moses advocates for the Israelites' freedom, opposing everything Pharaoh controls. Pharaoh keeps the Israelite people enslaved while he turns his head and indulges in his wealth. He has a hardened, unsympathetic heart, and he insists on controlling Egypt, constructing the whole city around his desires and preferences. Pharaoh refuses to listen to multiple caveats from Moses, even when the cost is physically, emotionally, and visibly obvious to everyone. In the face of mass plagues and infestations, he remains closed and determined to keep control. He is hopelessly unyielding.

Only after his own son dies does Pharaoh finally let the people go. In my personal therapy journey that followed those lonely nights on my college campus, I felt like Moses, confronted with my own burning bush. My calling was first and foremost to walk a path of healing and to be honest with the people around me. Later, it became clear that I was called to offer therapy to others. Like Moses, I felt unequipped for the tasks God had set before me. When I resorted to damning the warnings from others, I felt like Pharaoh clinging to my control of my own little Egypt. My therapy journey involved intermittent little Egypts and burning bushes. My efforts to control my little Egypts were familiar and self-validating but ultimately unhealthy. So I continued in waves of familiar, negative behaviors until a burning bush directed me back toward God's way of life.

Little Egypts represent the host of circumstances in our lives that we have the illusion of being able to control. Some of us attempt to control our food and weight. I had to confront the fact that my efforts to control weight and food during college were not a source of health management but an internal prison that kept me trapped in a life that limited rather than freed me. I accepted instead that I would need to navigate uncertainty and be willing to expose the unpredictable emotions and confusing, conflicted parts of myself. I had to get to know myself, for better or for worse. I let the vulnerable parts of myself be known in trusted relationships. As I did, I began to have glimpses of a new kind of experience, one where my spiritual needs are met, so my emotional ups and downs have room to move around more freely.

When I start grasping for Pharaoh-like control, I seek to let go a little more and acknowledge God's presence in my life. Moses took off his shoes and acknowledged the holy calling of the burning bush. Sometimes my burning bush is a passage of scripture that grounds me in the call to love rather than to control. Sometimes my burning bush is the voice of a friend or my therapist reminding me that I can let go of the illusion of perfection. Letting go of control and insistence on our own ways allows our hearts to open to possibilities that we may never have imagined. When we cling to our own little Egypts, we grasp for but do not find what we crave. But the Bible can show us how to take an active role in our faith without demanding control over every aspect.

We all have a calling from God—not a calling to orchestrate and maintain our little Egypts but a calling to quiet ourselves and look internally toward God's gentle but clear guidance. If we pause long enough, we may hear a gentle prompt, see a burning bush, and embrace a purposeful path. From that place of inward stillness we can cease being Pharaohs in charge of our little Egypts. We can let go.

Read Exodus 3:1-12; 11:9-10; 12:21-32. Ask yourself three questions: How do I see myself in this story? What is this story teaching me about myself? So what?

Thorns

When I am weak, then I am strong.

—2 Corinthians 12:10 (NIV)

Dusty and I live in a residential area of Atlanta with three young boys. We are often overcommitted, distracted, and too consumed with other responsibilities to pay much attention to the haphazard collection of trees, bushes, and ivy along our back fence. One day, when I ventured into the back corner of the yard, I walked into some small branches with sharp thorns on them. The branches were not dangerous or intimidating, but it was not long before I felt the sharp stick of a couple of thorns that really hurt. The thorns made me stop in my tracks and attempt to untangle myself. As I pulled away one branch, another seemed to grab hold of me. Some thorns embedded themselves into my sweatshirt, while others poked and scratched my skin. It took much longer than I expected to pry myself free of the entanglement into which I had wandered.

Spiritual and psychological thorns in our lives can be just as entangling. The thorns that cling to me now tend to be the nagging, residual demands of perfectionism and the need for achievement. Though I have come a long way in my personal journey, I still feel the stick of a thorn when I adopt impossibly high standards for myself or neglect self-compassion.

During college, the pain from my thorns was at its worst. My declared majors and body image shifted faster than the Ohio seasons. To cope, I sought relationships, substances, and social activities and became preoccupied with my weight and food intake. All of these distractions offered emotional numbness and gave me a brief respite from my uncomfortable and unsettled inner emotional landscape. But before long I would feel another thorn poking uncomfortably into my life. The thorns came in many forms: unsettling memories, waves of self-criticism, or the sting of perceived rejection in relationships. I tried tirelessly to remove each thorn myself, but inevitably another imbedded itself into my most vulnerable emotional places. My thorns pulled me outside of myself, away from any semblance of self-image as a child of God. The thorns took on a life of their own and entangled me in a place that took much longer than expected to resolve. I was smart, strong, and capable; but I couldn't seem to free myself.

During my sophomore year in college, I met weekly with my Bible study leader to discuss life from a spiritual perspective. Sincere and energetic, she was one of the stars of the Christian group on campus. If they had a prom court for the organization, she and her boyfriend would have been the queen and king. Although I attended the Christian group regularly, went on a couple of their retreats, and even led a Bible study for freshmen women, I somehow felt separate from the rest of the group. I wasn't as morally polished. Their excessive preoccupation with a set of norms and rules for dating, drinking, and life in general seemed restrictive and extreme to me. I kept feeling like there must be a way to honor God that was more freeing and fun.

Feeling morally inferior, I was surprised when my Bible study leader asked me to speak at an upcoming meeting where people would be sharing what God had done in their lives during spring break. I checked to make sure she remembered that I did not go on a mission trip. I reflected on my spring break, which I spent in St. Petersburg, Florida, with a group of friends. I thought about our night out with a group of Canadian guys and the shots we did at a club in Clearwater. I recalled my feelings of isolation in the hotel bathroom as I continued to battle my struggles with eating. I wondered if I could be anything more than an example of what *not* to do on spring break.

Hundreds of students would be attending the meeting. I asked my leader who else would be speaking, and she named a handful of prominent smiling Christians who had all been on mission trips to various parts of the world. Then she asked if I would be willing to share some brief thoughts on my struggles with eating along with my spring break story. She had a sense that there would be a lot of people who would relate. She sensed my reluctance and asked me to pray about it. I agreed, but I had a distinct suspicion that "praying about it" would consist of my feeling a crescendo of guilt until I agreed to do it. At the time, I assumed that God's path for me would be the most difficult and uncomfortable route. But I also had a sense that sharing an honest struggle could benefit someone, so I considered it.

I agreed to do the talk and began working on what to say. I tried to think of something that sounded spiritual with a quick brush past my struggles with eating in the last ten seconds of the talk. Maybe I could talk about the ocean being big like God? But that version of the talk felt disturbingly incomplete, empty, and dishonest.

The day approached and I had knots in my stomach every time I imagined myself on stage, a misfit among the moral and uncorrupt. I imagined the others' stories of saved souls, service projects, and love for the Lord in sharp contrast to my cycle of pain and purging from which I felt helpless to emerge. I started to cry. Soon I found myself on my knees on the floor of my dorm room. I was at the end of my own efforts, unsure what else to do, so it seemed fitting to pray. No clouds parted and no angels sang, but in my feelings of total incompetence, I knew without a doubt that God was with me.

The night came and, as I predicted, the first two talks were both shiny and impressive stories of fabulous missions trips and saved souls. My anxiety escalated, so I closed my eyes and asked God for help. A miraculous sense of peace came over me, and I wasn't scared anymore. I suddenly knew that God would give me the words I needed. I set aside my prepared talk and stepped onto the stage. An aura of calm centeredness enveloped me, and I began speaking the exact truth. I said that I would rather talk about God being as big as the ocean and say really spiritual stuff, but that I could not. I told the crowded room of people that I felt overwhelmed, stuck, and discouraged with more questions than answers about God. I wondered aloud why I seemed so stuck in a repetitive pattern of struggle, despite prayer and Bible study. I wondered what I had done wrong to deserve such powerfully painful emotions and why I continued to do so many things that I did not want to be doing. I named my thorns.

In order to experience the healing peace of God's constant presence, we have to learn to name, address, and sometimes even embrace our thorns. In his second letter to the Corinthians, the apostle Paul writes about his struggle with an unnamed thorn. Paul has an extreme, dynamic personality that leads him to assert boldly his views to those who oppose him. Before his dramatic experience on the road to Damascus, Paul condones the jailing and killing of Christians. (See Acts 8:1-3.) It takes no less than a personal confrontation and a blinding light from heaven to convince Paul that Jesus is the Messiah. Paul then writes and speaks about many personal experiences of faith. He refers to an unnamed "thorn" in his flesh (2 Cor. 12:7). Paul's thorn is such an intense burden to him that he pleads with God relentlessly to remove it, but God insists that Paul learn that God's grace is sufficient to allow Paul and his thorn to coexist. Divine power can be made perfect through human weakness.

I concluded my talk that night with the passage about Paul's thorn. My voice and hands shook as I read from my Bible: "For when I am weak, then I am strong" (2 Cor. 12:10, NIV). As I acknowledged the truth, it brought me onto steady ground in the arms of God, a true respite from the struggle. In that moment of vulnerability I discovered strength. If I could point to and acknowledge my thorns, their painful stick seemed to let up a little. I could enter into conversations of truth with my friends and therapist rather than hiding in the silences of feigned fine-feeling and behaviors that masked pain.

The thorns in each of our hearts present themselves in various ways. They are the core conflicts within us about our self-image, our relationships, and our ways of making sense of the world around us. They are behaviors or psychological realities that hinder our growth in faith and in life. But when we realize that God is greater than our thorns, especially amid our worst entanglements, God's power can break through. We can come to understand that our thorns may help reveal our greatest strengths. My own struggle through the muck of self-criticism and perfectionism resulted in a passion for helping other people overcome their own eating disorders. My own recovery has given me strength and determination to break through fear and sit with other people's discomfort and tension and uncertainty in the same way I had to sit with my own. God can use our voice, no matter our thorns, to work for good in the world.

Acknowledging and experiencing our thorns is a painful and refreshing process. When we feel the stick of a thorn, it jolts us into reality. Addressing thorns means tolerating and acknowledging their presence and the pain that they cause. But if we can embrace them, thorns can lead us to our greatest potential to share God's power with the world. Jesus offers his presence as we sit with the pain of each thorn and allow each thorn to coexist with us. Giving that talk during college marked an important step of faith for me. Many struggles followed, but that night I spoke to myself as well as the people listening as I acknowledged and validated my pain instead of glossing over it. In that validation, I experienced healing, and at least one thorn lost its control over me.

Read 2 Corinthians 12:1-10. Ask yourself three questions: How do I see myself in this story? What is this story teaching me about myself? So what?

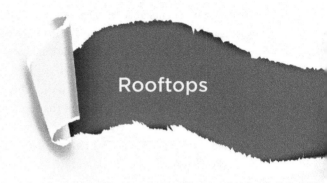

Rooftops

At the window of my house I looked out through my lattice, and I saw among the simple ones, I observed among the youths, a young man without sense, passing along the street near her corner, taking the road to her house in the twilight, in the evening, at the time of night and darkness.

—Proverbs 7:6-9

One atypically warm winter day during graduate school, I seized the opportunity to go out for a run. I rounded a familiar corner and felt an unfamiliar but compelling prompt rising up within me, urging me to walk. I was striving to improve my running pace at the time so I tried to push the prompt from my mind, but it persisted. In an annoyed sort of curiosity, I slowed to a walk. I sensed God's voice saying, "Slow down." I quickly realized God's prompting was not only about my running routine but also about my life. While my struggles with eating remained mostly in the rearview mirror, I continued to wrestle with perfectionism and unrealistically high standards for myself. As I continued the rest of my route home at a fast walking pace, some energy and clarity surfaced. I realized I had taken on too many school-related commitments.

During graduate school, I was high on achievement, driven to accomplish and acquire as many experiences as I could possibly get and to learn as much as I possibly could. Achievement was my first and foremost priority, and I excelled at it. No matter what I accomplished, I remained unsettled and discontent with myself, believing I had not yet done enough. I sought to fill any available space with the fraction of my energy that was yet unscheduled. I was teaching, supervising, seeing clients at several locations, and participating on additional treatment teams, all on top of a full course load of demanding classes. I rarely saw my husband, Dusty, as he also worked multiple jobs in addition to his own graduate course load.

My fast walk became a slower walk. Dusty and I had a discussion soon thereafter and came to an agreement that each of us would reduce our commitments by three immediately. I told one of the treatment teams that I could not continue. He stopped working an early-morning job to get adequate rest. We made other similar resolutions, and we found some breathing room in our lives. Our relationship had space to continue thriving; we could once again enjoy spontaneous moments together and had room to reflect on the gratitude we felt for each other and the opportunities graduate school offered.

When our lives are so full that we lose the ability to slow down, we can find ourselves on rooftops of discontent. David stands as a hero of the Christian faith, king of Israel and supposed author of many poetic Psalms. But David wanders near his own personal corner of destruction, driven by his discontent and desire. Maybe he is struggling with insecurities despite being king. Or maybe he feels entitled and deserving of whatever and whomever he wants. Second Samuel 11:2-4 tells us of David's wandering on his rooftop of discontent: "One evening David got up from his bed and walked around on the roof of the palace. From the roof he saw a woman bathing. The woman was very beautiful, and David sent someone to find out about her. The man said, 'She is Bathsheba, the daughter of Eliam and the wife of Uriah the Hittite.' Then David sent messengers to get her" (NIV).

In moments of impulsivity, David calls for Bathsheba, sleeps with her, and has her husband moved to the front lines of battle where he will be killed. He envies, covets, and has a man killed. As he seeks the woman on his neighbor's roof, David yearns to satisfy a sexual desire. In a series of mindless choices, he sacrifices spiritual peace and walks right into a seductive corner of self-destruction, taking Uriah and Bathsheba's marriage down with him in the process. He feels a common thirst and seeks to quench it with his own methods, damning the cost to other people, and lodges another rock into the void between himself and God.

Bathsheba's feelings about the event are curiously absent from the story. Does she welcome the invitation? Is it forceful? We do not know. We only know that King David sends for her, and King David gets what he wants. Many biblical heroes have serious lapses in judgment and stray from wisdom. Moses murders a man in rage. (See Exodus 2:11-12.) Peter cuts off a man's ear with a sword. (See John 18:10.) Lot gets so drunk that he passes out and fails to notice his daughters sleeping with him in a desperate attempt to preserve the family line. (See Genesis 19:30-36.) Countless Israelites worship the idol of the golden calf. (See Exodus 32:1-8.) All the Bible's heroes have both their shining moments and their thorns. Just like us.

We all covet what we do not have. The Ten Commandments indicate that God knows that humans covet. Perhaps God commands us not to covet our neighbor's spouse or belongings because God anticipates the suffering we experience when we act impulsively in response to our feelings. God's commandments challenge us to live out of contentment rather than in constant want. Yet our culture infects us with a state of material thirst and want that crowds out the possibilities for contentment. We relish the brief shot of dopamine in our brains when we buy and get and own. It's a tiny dose of shopping cocaine, and we justify it again and again.

We all have felt the pull toward something shiny and appealing that promises more than it can deliver, and we have been burned when it leaves us wanting. Proverbs 7 tells of a young man who wanders near the corner of a seductress, whom the author portrays as an alluring female figure on the street beckoning persuasively to the young man. For some of us, this personification of seduction represents an actual person. For others, she stands in the place of a substance or unhealthy vice: a compulsion to exercise, clean, count, or restrict food. She may personify our pursuit of a perfect body or the controlled appearance of a perfectly decorated home. We may be seduced by the unquenchable need for achievement or wealth. Whatever our seductions, they are attractive and infectious and seem to be the answer to our deep spiritual thirst. David sees a woman bathing on a roof, but his seduction exists within his own heart. The seductress in Proverbs 7 offers a personification of anything that pulls us from devotion to God and seduces us in a harmful way. She represents the addictive and seductive pull of our own desires that distract us from relationships and the fulfilling life God intends for us. David is seduced by the idea of having whatever he wants without limit, the power to breach the boundaries of marriage to have sex with a beautiful married woman. In his rooftop moment of discontent, he takes for granted all he has and feels entitled to more.

Before telling the story of the seduced young man, Proverbs 7 begins with a warning, a command to prevent our own destruction. The author urges us to keep God's words of truth stored up within our hearts. God's command is not to pretend that our seductions do not exist or to pretend that we are not tempted by their appeal. Keeping truth in our hearts is not about checking off a list of religious rituals but engaging in truth in a way that permeates our desires. It involves an intentional, serious transformation of our heart and an orientation toward God. By turning our heart toward God we can satisfy our thirst and deal with the temptation from our personal seductions.

The young man described in Proverbs 7 feels the pull of a seductress. Before he takes the first step, he has an opportunity to be more self-aware and reflective about where he is going, what he wants, and what he needs. Each step fuels momentum toward the next step. We are wise to understand what prompts our own initial steps toward situations and relationships we'd be better off without. We may become restless, looking for more excitement, passion, or entertainment in lives that lack joy. So we reach for a strong drink or a numbing comfort food, or we dial a number that would best be deleted from our phone's contact list. We do not need to become too creative in providing our own rationalization for the behaviors in which we are about to engage. Our seductions are happy to do so for us: "My husband is not at home; he has gone on a long journey. He took his purse filled with money and will not be home till full moon" (Prov. 7:19-20, NIV). We can place the blame anywhere but on ourselves when we make the decision to engage with our seductions. The man in Proverbs 7 follows his seductress "like an ox to the slaughter" (Prov. 7:22). His decision will cost him his life. Our lack of joy may prompt us to take initial steps toward a relationship that seems to promise more joy but offers only momentary pleasure. Wisdom warns us in no uncertain terms: "Do not let your hearts turn aside to her ways; do not stray into her paths. For many are those she has laid low, and numerous are her victims. Her house is the way to Sheol, going down to the chambers of death" (Prov. 7:25-27). Eventually, stepping forward with a lack of mindfulness will put us in a compromising position.

When we are so driven that we lose sight of contentment, we may find ourselves on rooftops of discontent, just as David did. When we experience discontent, we can make conscious decisions about how to respond. We can slow down and reflect on what we already have attained and accomplished with a perspective of gratitude. Decisions about what to do with our discontent continue as long as we live. We are wise to recognize and address discontent when it surfaces because our seductions will also be waiting in various forms. They will be quick to remind us of our special relationship with them. Like the seductress, our seductions quickly make it personal and give us a sense that we are unique and special: "So I came out to meet you; I looked for you and have found you!"

(Prov. 7:15, NIV). Her warm embrace so closely mimics God's love for us that it becomes difficult to resist.

Fortunately for his own sense of spiritual peace, David comes around. Psalm 51 may be David's song of repentance after his encounter with Bathsheba and after the murder of Bathsheba's husband Uriah: "Create in me a pure heart, O God, and renew a steadfast spirit within me. Do not cast me from your presence or take your Holy Spirit from me. Restore to me the joy of your salvation and grant me a willing spirit, to sustain me" (Ps. 51:10-12, NIV).

Rooftops and corners will always be present but so will the forgiving love of God and people who want to help us get back on track. We can practice gratitude for God's gifts and for the blessing of our family and friends. Some people practice gratitude by keeping a daily journal of small things they are thankful for at the beginning or end of each day. Such gratitude can keep us from discontent. When you need to, slow down and walk. Return to gratitude and a doable pace of contentment. When you do, you'll find less need to follow tempting distractions, and more capacity for a self-aware, spiritually focused path.

Read 2 Samuel 11. Ask yourself three questions: How do I see myself in this story? What is this story teaching me about myself? So what?

Almost

> *Thomas (who was called the Twin), one of the twelve, was not with them when Jesus came. So the other disciples told him, "We have seen the Lord." But he said to them, "Unless I see the mark of the nails in his hands, and put my finger in the mark of the nails and my hand in his side, I will not believe."*
>
> —John 20:24-25

When my oldest son, Carlson, was about eighteen months old, I found out I was pregnant again. I was thrilled. I began to envision a family with two children, siblings who could play with each other. For a month, I could see it so clearly in my mind. The two little ones would laugh and play and, of course, get along. I would sip my coffee from a comfortable chair and call to them when it was time for dinner. They would playfully race one another to the table, where they'd gratefully eat what I'd prepared. After dinner, one would offer to share his Lego bricks, and the other would hug him. I was not completely naive. I knew another baby would present some challenges. But my first pregnancy unfolded with so few difficulties and such a joyous outcome that I completely took it for granted. I assumed my second would be fine too.

However, around seven weeks into my pregnancy, I noticed concerning signs that I was miscarrying. In a panicked daze, I approached a coworker as my fearful tears surfaced. She immediately offered help and said she would cover my therapy groups that evening. I drove home and began to feel the stab of loss along with a lingering hope that maybe it would somehow not really be true. I called my doctor, who told me to come in the next morning or to call if the pain got worse. I slept fitfully, tossing and turning while my hope dissipated and my skepticism grew. I knew what was happening, but when I got an ultrasound that confirmed it, I was devastated. I tried to absorb the nurse's words: "There is no pregnancy in the uterus."

My miscarriage happened three days before Thanksgiving in 2008. I sat in the car on the long drive from Georgia to Ohio with layers of compounding grief. I tried to piece together and reconstruct my visions for the future. A nagging, unsettling fear of future losses churned in my gut. *Would my vision of siblings come to pass? Had I done something wrong? Why would God allow this to happen?* Several of my friends were pregnant at the same time. One had the same due date. I have met those children, and I still think about my own child that could have been.

When something good *almost* happens, we experience a spiritually uncomfortable type of grief. There is a glaring absence of an event we hoped would come to pass. There's a great event that other people got to experience but, for some reason, we have missed out on. Something good has happened; we could have been there, experienced that, but we did not. So we blame or question or utterly doubt God. We ask, "Why did this experience pass me by? Where in God's plan does it make sense for me *not* to experience this good thing?" It may be a relationship that didn't become a marriage or a marriage that we thought would be better than it is. It may be a particular parenting moment we've always envisioned and assumed would occur. It may be a career opportunity that seemed like a sure thing, and now the door is closed. We've hoped and prayed for something, and it hasn't occurred. Worse yet, it seems to be happening effortlessly for others.

How do we make sense of our circumstances when something we expected to bring good to our lives has not come to pass? How do we reconcile this reality with our beliefs that God should provide protection and peace? These are the questions I imagine Jesus' disciple Thomas asking after Jesus' first appearance to the disciples after his resurrection, when every disciple was present other than Thomas. (See John 20:19-25.) It must have been a Spirit-filled moment of elation and celebration. I imagine Thomas asking himself for the next week, "Why did Jesus show up when I was the only one not there? Surely, being God, he could have chosen a time when all of us were present. This feels personal."

Maybe Thomas's doubts about Jesus are not so much about whether Jesus is the Son of God, but why, being the Son of God, he would show up when Thomas is not there, for everyone else but him. It must sting. A miraculous reconciling experience has happened without Thomas. For a week, he has to listen to the rest of the disciples talk about Jesus' appearance to all of them while he feels like the odd one out. Thomas has to sit with the fact that he *almost* saw Jesus. He must wonder why he had been excluded from that moment. I can imagine John turning to Thomas to reminisce and realizing awkwardly that Thomas cannot share the memory. Thomas hadn't been there. I wonder if the other disciples offer any explanations to Thomas about why Jesus may have appeared in Thomas's absence, and what those explanations might be. I wonder where Thomas is and what he is doing when he misses Jesus.

You may also relate to Thomas's feelings about almost experiencing something good, almost seeing Jesus. Have you ever had that isolated feeling in your faith where others around you, even those closest to you, seem to have been present for some experience of God that you missed? Thomas could determine that God is leaving him out. We all struggle to interpret God's actions through our time-limited, cloudy lens. We can be sure that Jesus knows Thomas fully. Maybe Jesus knows that Thomas needs a separate revelation. Maybe something about the opportunity to touch Jesus' hand and side provides the intensely physical and uniquely unforgettable revelation that Thomas needs.

Thomas is an inquisitive and trusting disciple, willing to follow Jesus wherever he goes. But, like all of us, he has doubts. Amid his doubt, Thomas cannot imagine the rest of the story, the events that have not yet played out. Jesus, who may seem to forget about or disregard Thomas, has planned a revelation just for him. It is not in the timing or the way that Thomas expects: "A week later his disciples were again in the house, and Thomas was with them. Although the doors were shut, Jesus came and stood among them and said, 'Peace be with you.' Then he said to Thomas, 'Put your finger here and see my hands. Reach out your hand and put it in my side. Do not doubt but believe.' Thomas answered him, 'My Lord and my God!'" (John 20:26-28).

Thomas first looks at others' experience of Jesus to determine his own belief. Yet spiritual comparisons often are unhelpful. We may not experience the revelation of Jesus in the same way or the same timing as the person sitting next to us, and that is OK. Thomas's disbelief does not alarm Jesus. Jesus doesn't rush back to reassure Thomas that he is indeed the risen Christ. He lets Thomas sit with his unbelief for a while and recognizes the value in holding off from immediate reassurance. When Jesus says to Thomas, "Do not doubt but believe" (John 20:27), he may allude to the truth of his own identity. But that point is probably obvious by the time Thomas touches the physical evidence of Jesus' wounds. Jesus' words urging Thomas to believe may address Thomas's lingering disbelief about Jesus' timing. Jesus may be telling Thomas to believe in God's timing and methods as well as in his identity as the risen Christ.

When Jesus says, "Blessed are those who have not seen and yet have come to believe" (John 20:29), I wonder whether he speaks not only to those who have not seen Jesus in his resurrected bodily form but also to those who have not yet seen all of what Jesus will do in their lives. Many persons have not yet seen how and when Jesus will reveal himself to them. Even those of us who have experienced Jesus in some way sit with uncertainty about when and if it will happen again.

Our purpose in God's plan unfolds over time. It is a process. Jesus seems to be saying to all of us, "Blessed are those who have not yet seen what I am about to do, and yet believe I am going to do something good and powerful in their lives." This ongoing truth applies not just to seeing Jesus with our eyes but also to recognizing Jesus' work in our lives with a wise, Spirit-given perception that trusts that Jesus fully knows us. When we cannot make sense of things through our own limited perspective, we can rest in Jesus' words, "Peace be with you. . . . Do not doubt but believe" (John 20:26-27).

When I had the miscarriage, I did not know what God had in store. I did not appreciate that having just one miscarriage was a gift. I now have three boys, and my experience of loss has contributed to my gratefulness for the three pregnancies that resulted in Carlson, Caleb, and Zach. Now, I cannot imagine our family any other way. I can embrace my experience of loss because it has made me intensely grateful for the children I have. I also am grateful that I was not further along in the pregnancy I lost. I can understand other women's losses, and I feel deep compassion for women with similar stories of loss who are still waiting for a better outcome. Yet at the same time, I still grieve.

God knows us fully and sees the long-term perspective on our lives that we cannot see. God reveals God to Thomas in the way he needs to see God. God does the same for each of us. When we cannot understand what God is doing, or why, we can be filled with the peace God freely offers. God reminds us of the nuanced way of revelation, personal and well-timed for each of us.

Read John 20:11-29. Ask yourself three questions: How do I see myself in this story? What is this story teaching me about myself? So what?

Weeping

When Mary came where Jesus was and saw him, she knelt at his feet and said to him, "Lord, if you had been here, my brother would not have died." When Jesus saw her weeping, and the Jews who came with her also weeping, he was greatly disturbed in spirit and deeply moved. He said, "Where have you laid him?" They said to him, "Lord, come and see." Jesus began to weep.

—John 11:32-35

In the aftermath of grief and loss, Jesus weeps with us. When we think he's failed to show up, or his timing seems disturbingly off, his presence is one of overwhelming companionship and mutual weeping. He does not brush past the discomfort, and we don't need to, either. We need to grieve, and nothing is wrong or unhealthy about our faith when we do. In grieving deeply, despite reasons for eventual joy, we are following Jesus' example.

We grieve when people die. At times, we also grieve the loss of parts of ourselves. In 2017, countless allegations of sexual assault were directed at prominent men in leadership roles. Survivors of sexual assault started posting a powerful response on social media, and the #MeToo movement rapidly grew.[1] Survivors everywhere, in so many different yet strikingly similar scenarios, acknowledged their experiences of sexual harassment, abuse, and assault and raised awareness of just how many people have been affected by another's abusive violation of boundaries. According to the Rape, Abuse, and Incest National Network (RAINN), one out of every six women and one out of every thirty-three men are victims of an attempted or completed rape in their lifetime.[2] Sexual assault is not merely a traumatic event. Survivors face the challenge of trying to untangle a mass of resulting complicated emotions and beliefs. We navigate a long aftermath of working to overcome fear, shame, and self-doubt. We stumble through the dark alleys of the arduous healing process as we try to overcome intrusive memories of post-traumatic stress and reengage with life in a meaningful and less avoidant way.

For many on their journeys through healing from abuse and assault, it can seem like Jesus shows up too late, or not at all. Survivors may wonder if God is unconcerned with, removed from, or indifferent to their struggle. I've asked these questions myself through my own journey of healing. Does God allow, or even approve of, abuse and mistreatment? If God is so powerful, can't God stop such atrocities? If God is so full of love, how does God allow such pain? Is God passive? Incapable? Uncaring? These may be some of the most spiritually challenging questions we can ask, sit with, and continue to ask.

Mary must ask the same difficult questions when her beloved brother, Lazarus, dies. She and her sister, Martha, are close friends of Jesus. They've reached out to him, sent for him, pleaded for his help. So why does Jesus fail to show up when Lazarus is sick and dying? Jesus waits two days before heading in their direction to offer comfort and support. Amid great loss, when the living Christ is surely capable of preventing it, their brother Lazarus dies. They trust Jesus and call to Jesus. And for two days, Jesus remains devastatingly absent. (See John 11:1-14.)

The death of Lazarus looks different for each of us. Sometimes we call to Jesus and he does not show up in our preferred timing. Grief occurs not only when someone dies but also with any type of loss: the end of a relationship, the decline of health and capabilities as we age, the loss of a job, the loss of a carefree childhood, a major change in career path, or an unrealized dream or expectation. All of these experiences involve grief.

In grief, we lose sight of the resurrection and restoration that we know is coming. Lazarus will be brought back to life; Mary and Martha will hug him, be close to him, and laugh with him again. But in the painful interim, the tardy Jesus appears and does the unexpected. He does not enact immediate restoration. Instead, he weeps. He consoles the grief-stricken Mary and Martha. Surely Jesus of all people could allow them to skip the grief and get straight to the coming miracle. He could say, "It's okay, Mary. Don't worry, Martha. I'm going to help and heal, and Lazarus is going to come back to life. Everyone can feel better now." He could bring immediate joy, hope, and restoration to the occasion and relieve everyone's grief on a more preferred time line. But he does not. He sits with them and weeps in prolonged discomfort and pain. He knows perfectly well that an exciting outcome lies ahead, but he chooses not to provide it just yet. Assuming Jesus lives a life of perfected love, could it be that there is value in allowing for and sitting with grief without rushing to resurrection as the ultimate consolation?

We would do well to learn from Jesus' example, to allow time for grief and to embrace and value it. When we grieve alongside a friend or family member when a loved one dies, we build an intimate connection. We absorb and share in a deep sadness of never being able to embrace our loved one again. We take a mutual glance at our own mortality and acknowledge our sacred and ephemeral lives. We embrace one another a little longer, more grateful for those who remain in our lives, and promise ourselves not to take them for granted. It's possible that Lazarus's death opens the door for Mary and Martha to be even more connected to Jesus.

The story of faith includes heartache; but it also includes resurrection, restoration, and life. There is hope and joy through Jesus in an eternal sense and in the life and death story of Lazarus. It is equally true that resurrection is coming for those who have been assaulted. The part of each person that dies during an assault can be restored and brought back to life. That part can live as Lazarus lives after the weeping and grief have had time to run their course.

When we think that Jesus misses the mark and should take another mode of intervention in our lives, we can know that he weeps with us. In doing so, we may be able to sit in his embrace a while longer and feel less isolated while he acknowledges our losses with us before moving on to a joyful conclusion that may minimize or gloss over our pain if it arrived too soon. We do enough to minimize the pain within ourselves, and we can benefit from making space for grief and expanding our hearts to feel our losses acutely and fully. In doing so, we begin to heal.

Our losses may always hold a sting. After Lazarus's resurrection, Mary and Martha may still sit with unanswered questions about Jesus' timing, plan, and methods. Martha says to Jesus, "Lord, if you had been here, my brother would not have died" (John 11:21). She and Mary may wonder whether Jesus could have thought through it a bit more and intervened on a time line that was a better fit for them.

The joy of resurrection does not minimize pain, but allows full permission for it. Jesus shows us that there is no rush to hurry through the uncomfortable, wounded places in our journey. Rather, Jesus is present to be still with us, weep with us, and sit with us for as long as it takes. Each tear he sheds for us flows in a way that validates and carries us through our losses.

Read John 11:1-44. Ask yourself three questions: How do I see myself in this story? What is this story teaching me about myself? So what?

WEEKEND PRACTICE

Journaling for Self-Awareness

This week, we revisited Jesus' announcement and call to an internal journey of self-awareness and healing. As we delve into our journey of self-reflection, we are learning to set aside what others are doing and expecting of us in this moment to pause and connect with Jesus in self-reflection.

This weekend, you'll use a journal as a tool for this work. I urge you to use your journal throughout your reading of this book to delve deeper into your human experience with its wide range of spiritual and emotional waves. If you already journal regularly, continue to do so in the ways that work for you. If you have never consistently used a journal, get one. It can be a basic notebook or something more decorative and elaborate. The externals don't matter except in the ways that they are important to you and your internal process. Maybe you'll choose a simple notebook, or maybe you'll choose something with a meaningful symbol.

If you are starting a new journal, copy down your Modern Creed as your first entry. Find a place to keep your journal where you can quickly grab it and jot down observations, thoughts, and feelings. Allow yourself to let go of neatness, grammar, and spelling. There will not be a required length for any entry. Sometimes you may draw a picture or scribble in a particular color that represents what you feel. Journals are a tool for facilitating self-expression and self-awareness. Consider using pictures, symbols, colors, and different types of pens or pencils. Trust yourself, and honor your preferences. But do some journaling every day.

Creating a Time Line

Take some time this weekend to explore and reflect on the events of your life thus far. Identify your desert experiences of *Thorns*, *Rooftops*, and *Weeping*, note instances when you seek control through your *Little Egypts*, and recall times when you *Almost* got what you wanted. In your journal, try the following practice.

1. On a blank page or sheet of paper, make a long line representing the years of your life, from birth to present day.
2. Label experiences on the time line that represent "desert" experiences, next to the age when they occurred. Desert experiences are times when you've felt distant from God or when you have faced particularly difficult challenges.
3. Look at your time line. Prayerfully consider what further steps of healing God may be prompting you to take. Do you need to talk to someone, let go of an offense, or seek forgiveness?
4. In light of your painful experiences, what would it mean to come to Jesus and to look for ways God is revealing truth to you?
5. Make a commitment to take one step this weekend to seek further spiritual growth in relation to the deserts you have known.

In taking these steps, you are practicing self-awareness and self-expression through journaling. Journaling can also be used for setting goals. My last challenge for you for this weekend practice is to set one goal for yourself for the remainder of this study given what you've learned about yourself through journaling about the questions above. Write the goal in your journal, and pray for God to walk with you as you persevere toward your goal.

If you are new to journaling and would like a bit of structure, experiment with the following exploring needs exercise. Even if you have journaling habits you love that you will continue in your daily practice throughout the rest of your time with this book, try this prompt sometime this week in light of the time line you worked on this weekend.

Exploring Needs

1. Write the word *revealed* or *revelation*. Then write about any thoughts, feelings, or experiences that you associate with that word.
2. Then make a list of the ways you seek fulfillment. These may include a behavior, a hobby, or some type of work. These also may include a particular achievement, a particular financial goal, or a particular person's approval. Try only to identify rather than evaluate.
3. Ask yourself, *When I am aware of my pain, what do I most need?* It may be that you need validation or comfort or reassurance or companionship. Maybe you need confidence, love, or respect. Consider a few ways that those needs can be met, and take one step this weekend toward meeting one of those needs in a healthy way that values you and your process of healing and growth.

WEEK THREE: WHERE YOU FIND TRUTH

Retreats

Lord, you have been our dwelling place in all generations. Before the mountains were brought forth, or ever you had formed the earth and the world, from everlasting to everlasting you are God.
—Psalm 90:1-2

The alarm on the bedside table next to me sounded in a repetitive, nagging beep at 3:50 a.m. I quickly washed my hands and face and brushed my teeth. In jeans and a hoodie, I walked down a long hallway. Still in a half-asleep daze, I descended a stairwell, opened a heavy door, and entered the Abbey Church for a 4:00 a.m. Vigils service at The Monastery of the Holy Spirit in Conyers, Georgia. I found a seat on a wooden pew on the side of the Abbey as a loud chime signaled the beginning of the service. I felt an intense calm in the quiet, austere Abbey and its simplistic reverence. It stands tall with curved, white beams that extend upward on each side of the Abbey and come to a point at the top of the ceiling. The beams felt to me like the fingers of God, and I sat securely in God's hands as I prayed.

That weekend I was on a two-day retreat, from Friday evening to around noon on Sunday. The experience offered a great deal of silence and solitude. Periodically throughout the weekend, I attended talks in the conference room of the retreat house given by the monks. The monks spoke about the importance of prayer. One of the senior monks sat hunched over in his chair and spoke about his life of ministry, which included trips to Africa. He spoke from a place of deep wisdom, slowly and thoughtfully, like a Catholic Yoda. He urged us with solemn words to *pray in the middle of the night*. I wondered silently if there couldn't possibly be some other important takeaway from the weekend, but I sensed in the urgency with which he spoke, after so many years of prayer and service, that he was sharing a deep, central truth.

I attended prayer services in the Abbey Church up to five times a day, beginning with the Vigils service at 4:00 a.m. and concluding with a Compline service at 7:30 p.m. I chanted the psalms with the monks, sang hymns, and listened to teachings from scripture. I sat with other retreat attendees separate from the monks but close enough to sense their deep devotion to the art and practice of prayer. Halfway through the Vigils, there is a solid half hour of complete silence and reflection. During that time, the monks and retreat attendees are free to move about the Abbey to find a quiet corner or pew where we can engage in focused prayer. Something about that silent movement into my own focused place ushered me into God's presence even more. The Abbey's quiet beauty holds a distinct appeal: Monks read scripture readings in a reverent but controlled, monotone voice. Yet the words echo powerfully throughout the room to be received by attentive listeners. The scriptures came alive for me in a distraction-free way that they never had before. I've since attended several weekend retreats at the monastery, and the Vigils service is always my favorite. Getting up to pray at such an early hour connects me to Jesus, who repeatedly sought God in prayer. Praying at that time, in that place, reinforces for me the experience of being alone, but alone with God.

On my first visit to the monastery, I was in my mid-thirties, navigating life as a new parent and trying to balance family and career. My life involved a daily routine of packing lunches and snacks, scheduling and seeing clients, evaluating whether clients needed to be hospitalized, doing paperwork, attending team meetings, feeding children, reading to children, returning phone calls, and binge-watching Netflix until I fell asleep. I did not seek out the monastery because I'm monk-like. I heard that the retreat house would offer silence for an entire weekend, and I was sold. In a life that seemed in constant motion with little opportunity to pause, the monastery came as a welcome source of silence and spiritual refreshment. My mind took several hours to slow down, but as it did, I felt powerfully drawn to God within the walls of the retreat house. The silence encouraged a calmer mind, and I felt a greater sense of openness to hearing God's voice in my spirit. I discovered and recovered an experience of prayer that had been absent from my life for a long time.

There was a time when I felt church needed to be flashy and emotional with a compelling sermon presentation and a pastor with a well-trained speaking style. After meeting the monks, this was no longer the case. They offer a compelling simplicity in work, community, and devotion to God. They wear simple robes and have few personal possessions. They commit to living and working in a monastic community as brothers for life. They are incredibly tuned in and attentive to other people. It's as though the degree of stripping externals and possessions from their own lives has led to a special ability for them to see past our material baggage too.

During subsequent visits to the monastery, I was again pulled toward simplicity, prayer, and God's divine presence and direction in my life. I began to hear the voice of God prompting me to take retreats, not necessarily just to the monastery but also into the presence of God throughout my day and week regardless of my physical location.

The psalmist refers to God as "our dwelling place" (Ps. 90:1). Our dwelling place in God is more spiritual than physical, but it is just as real as the four walls that surround us. We can spend great time and energy creating, flipping, furnishing, buying, selling, renting, and decorating our residences. We would be wise to invest as much energy in cultivating a spiritual residence in God.

We often attribute characteristics of people to God. God can be understood as a parental figure, a friend, a spiritual counselor, or an advocate. We can also get to know God as a place, a refuge to which we can always return. Places like the monastery can provide a setting that facilitates our journey inward. We can find ourselves in a variety of environments that all have the potential to point us toward the inward spiritual and emotional work we need to do. That inward work is a prerequisite for outward signs of our faith.

The beams of the Abbey Church continue to come to my mind in moments of stress and uncertainty. When I lose perspective and feel spiritually stagnant, I can revisit the image of a constant, peaceful presence of God holding me in a loving and secure embrace. God's security is available regardless of the storms that rage outside the walls of the Abbey or inside my heart. In God's security, I remember that God is with me and is willing to shine a healing light into the darkest and most complicated corners of my life.

Retreats can involve weekends away from life's usual routines or moments of prayer during the busiest days. Sometimes retreats happen when I park in a grocery store parking lot and take ten minutes to read a short devotional. I recenter myself spiritually and find comfort that relieves the pressure of needing to orchestrate my own life. Sometimes retreats happen when I awaken in the quiet of night and can muster the energy to get out of bed to pray and read a chapter of scripture. Just as the monk suggested, the hours in the middle of the night somehow allow the voice of God to come to us much more quickly and in powerful ways. In momentary retreats, I gain clarity about which efforts in my life are of the greatest value and significance. I can reorient my focus onto a meaningful path in God's presence. I believe this is the experience God desires us to have—whether in a monastery, lying in bed awake at night, or in any other place we happen to find ourselves searching for peace.

At first, I felt like I needed to have regular visits to the monastery as often as I could manage it, and I do take opportunities to revisit the peaceful environment there. But I eventually realized that at the monastery I found an internal place to which I repeatedly can return at any time. It's a place of peace where the concerns of life temporarily can be set aside to make room for God's revelation for my life. Our hearts are God's dwelling place. When we are still, we will find restoration there.

Read Psalm 90. Ask yourself three questions: How do I see myself in this story? What is this story teaching me about myself? So what?

Kihaps

The voice of the Lord breaks the cedars; the Lord breaks the cedars of Lebanon. . . . The voice of the Lord causes the oaks to whirl, and strips the forests bare; and in his temple all say, "Glory!"
—Psalm 29:5, 9

Kihap is a word made up of two smaller Korean words, *ki* and *hap*. *Ki* refers to our internal energy. *Hap* is an intense concentration and focus. A kihap is a loud yell voiced by Taekwondo martial artists as they strike a target. There are three reasons for doing a kihap. First, it startles your opponent and adds an element of intimidation. Second, sounding a kihap results in physically tightening the core of the body for a split second, adding power to a kick as you execute it. Third, a kihap is energizing and empowering. White belt students who are beginning Taekwondo often have to find their kihaps.

I sat on the edge of the mat and watched four-year-old Carlson kicking targets and yelling his kihap. I chased one-year-old Caleb around the edge of the mat as he vacillated between watching the practice, playing with my keys, and toddling onto the mat in an effort to join the class. Sometimes he would kick out his little toddler leg in an effort to kick like his big brother. Between my efforts to redirect and entertain him, I watched the students and noticed that both adults and children were training at the Taekwondo *dojang*. I reflected on my own brief study of Taekwondo during my senior year of college, when I earned a yellow belt and broke my first board. Graduate school and my first years of parenthood had crowded out any time for practicing Taekwondo. As I tuned in more to what Carlson learned during class, I longed to be a part of it again. I decided to sign up, and I began attending some classes on my own and some with Carlson. Several years later, I became a black belt in Taekwondo.

In preparation for the black belt test, I became anxious. I noticed tension in my shoulders as I struggled to execute kicks with the correct technique. My Taekwondo Master exhorted me to relax on many occasions. As I continued to prepare for belt tests, I felt a sense of impending pressure to perform well, to choose the best board-breaking demonstration I could successfully complete, and to execute each kick and punch as powerfully and accurately as possible. Such pressure led me to a state of tension and self-doubt. I continually revisited my need to relax.

One day, our Master paused between drills and called the students into a huddle for an instructional moment. He explained to us that the most explosive power in a kick is only possible when you start from a state of calm relaxation. He added that we would not get the explosive power needed for an effective kick when we started from a state of tension. I absorbed his feedback and practiced my kicks from a relaxed stance. I was startled at the power I exerted in my kicks when I started from a calm state. I kicked the target harder than ever.

It became clear to me that the need to remain calm is not only true in a physical sense but also in a spiritual sense. The practice of Taekwondo offers variety, challenge, and fun. I regularly kick targets, spar, yell, and break boards. During every class, I experience a therapeutic rush of endorphins, which leaves me in a calmer state than when I began. I regularly alternate between a relaxed state and a state of powerful execution. I have also spent a significant amount of time in therapy, spiritual study, and self-reflection. As a result, I recognize trials and pain as normal parts of life that need to be acknowledged. I know I need prayer and support from others to persevere. I need times to step away from excessive activity and commitments for rest and restoration. I alternate between times of spiritual challenge and spiritual rest.

In my personal therapy, I had to find my voice and identity and get comfortable making space for both. I had to accept that my feelings and preferences are valid and learn to assert and express myself more freely. The practice of my Taekwondo kihap now extends into my everyday life. Sounding a strong kihap with my life means being less fearful. It means persevering. I do not apologize for my presence or feelings. I claim some space and assert my presence. I know and value the perspective and expertise I can bring to a situation.

Sounding a spiritual kihap means asserting ourselves powerfully and allowing space in our spiritual lives to alternate between spiritual intensity and spiritual rest. Our lives bring storms, but Jesus can calm the storms that life presents to us. Loved ones die early and unexpectedly. Pregnancies are lost. Addictions take hold of the lives of those we love. Repeated intentions fail. Acute traumas leave us numb and speechless in their powerful wake, and long-term traumas erode our energy and self-confidence slowly over time. If we are not intentional about our time and resources, the small stressors of life can compound into an impossibly full calendar of responsibilities that seem to leave no room for larger goals. How are we to navigate these storms without churning in a constant state of tension? How can we execute a powerful spiritual kihap in our lives from such a tense state?

Jesus does not offer us a path without trouble. This life will present trouble and trials. However, he promises that alongside the trouble we will find peace that we cannot understand. Jesus is the vine, and if we remain in him as branches, we can bear fruit. (See John 15:1-7.) The fruit he speaks of is "love, joy, peace, patience, kindness, generosity, faithfulness, gentleness, and self-control" (Gal. 5:22-23). Tension, on the other hand, produces anger, stress, unrest, impatience, harshness, deception, and reactivity. Tension is both less effective and less powerful.

One way to experience spiritual restoration is through the practice of *lectio divina*, the sacred reading of scripture.[1] The practice involves reading scripture slowly and contemplatively until one phrase stands out. I rest on that phrase and write it down. I prayerfully repeat it and listen for what God may be revealing through the scripture. When I make time for this practice in the morning, I feel more focused and empowered throughout the rest of the day.

When we first connect to the vine and rest in a calm state, we discover energy and empowerment. The tension of temporal concerns no longer bogs us down. We cannot help becoming more focused and effective, because our energy naturally flows from our connection to Jesus. We can more powerfully assert our presence and purpose, like a powerful kick. The answer lies in starting from a calm state, connected to Jesus. When we remain in him, we thrive with explosive power to overcome challenges.

Being connected to the vine means tapping into the explosive power available to us through God and unleashing it from a calm state of peace. When we start with a calm state, we maximize our potential impact and power in our lives and communities. When we connect with Jesus, explosive spiritual power can work in us and flow into the lives of those around us.

Read Psalm 29. Ask yourself three questions: How do I see myself in this story? What is this story teaching me about myself? So what?

Donkeys

Then the Lord opened the mouth of the donkey, and it said to Balaam, "What have I done to you, that you have struck me these three times?" Balaam said to the donkey, "Because you have made a fool of me! I wish I had a sword in my hand! I would kill you right now!" But the donkey said to Balaam, "Am I not your donkey, which you have ridden all your life to this day? Have I been in the habit of treating you this way?" And he said, "No." Then the Lord opened the eyes of Balaam, and he saw the angel of the Lord standing in the road, with his drawn sword in his hand; and he bowed down, falling on his face.

—Numbers 22:28-31

I attended my first process therapy group during the summer after my freshman year of college. In process therapy groups, members are encouraged to talk about emotions. At the time, any discussion of emotions made me feel uncomfortable and exposed. The group began with a check-in process, and each group member was asked about feelings that were present in that moment. When my turn came, the group therapist looked at me expectantly. I was trying to make sense of my emotions that kept surfacing and felt unmanageable. I truly did not know how I felt. It seemed too complicated to put into words. The therapist pushed me to think a bit more about it and to come up with some type of emotion word. I said, "Good," and he looked at me kindly but as though he wanted to know more. He seemed to question for a moment whether to push me further. I imagine that he let my vague response slide since it was my first day in the group.

After the check-in, we stared blankly at the floor or other inanimate objects in the room for what seemed like two hours. Finally, I breathed a sigh of relief as the man sitting next to me broke the silence. He seemed so free and expressive as he talked about his feelings. I wished I could do the same, but I knew for certain that I could not. As he and some of the others talked, my thoughts started moving faster. Slowly, my feelings emerged and pushed me to express them. I didn't know what to do, so I pushed back, determined to suppress them. I feared what would happen if I voiced them, so I sat quietly through most of the group. For the entire duration of the process therapy group, I felt like crying but tried to contain my sadness. I simultaneously wanted to release my sadness and to maintain a sense of emotional control. When it was my turn to check out by identifying an emotion at the conclusion of the group, I just looked at the therapist and said I felt fine.

Balaam is a biblical master of divination who learns what it means to encounter unwelcome feelings and messages. He makes efforts to silence an unwelcome message in the same way that many of us seek to silence our emotional pain. Balaam has just been offered a well-paying job in service to Balak. He does not expect a voice of wisdom and resistance to come from his donkey.

Balak wants to avoid defeat by the Israelites, who have already been victorious in two other regions, so he seeks Balaam's help to foresee the future and stop the Israelites. Balaam accepts the job, but he decides to consult with the God of the Israelites. God warns Balaam not to help Balak, so Balaam declines Balak's offer. Balak then extends an even more generous offer if Balaam would help Balak defeat the Israelites. This time when Balaam consults with God, God allows Balaam to go to Balak but orders him to speak only as God tells him to speak.

During Balaam's journey, his donkey comes to an abrupt halt. Balaam has consulted with God and is following the path he feels is right for him. But the donkey refuses to budge any further down the path. Despite Balaam's forceful attempts to move his donkey forward, the donkey stays put. We have all felt Balaam's frustration. The donkey's one job is to carry him where he wants to go. However, the donkey is not the hindrance it appears to be. God enables the donkey to speak, and the donkey questions Balaam: "What have I done to you, that you have struck me these three times?" (Num. 22:28). The donkey can see an angel of the Lord with a drawn sword on the road ahead and wants to spare

Balaam's life. The donkey tries to protect Balaam. Balaam is known for powers of divination but cannot perceive the presence of danger inches from him. The donkey is so intent on protecting Balaam that he crushes Balaam's foot against a wall rather than continue on a path toward danger.

Balaam holds fast to his right to make his own decisions. He listens to and obeys God, but he still needs to learn to acknowledge that he can divine only what God allows him to divine. The donkey can see the angel right in front of them, but Balaam cannot see it until God allows him to see it. Balaam errs in beating his source of truth and protection because it is an unlikely vessel for God's voice. God's lesson for Balaam is not to get too attached to his own end goal. God has a plan for Balaam but asks for a moment-by-moment faith that honors what God asks Balaam to say and do. Balaam erupts with violent anger when unforeseen events interrupt his plan. The donkey that has carried him reliably will not budge.

We will certainly find our own versions of unexpected obstacles, even on paths we truly believe are from God. The car, house, plan, or relationship we thought was reliable begins to break down and look much different than we imagined it would. A career path takes an unexpected direction. A loved one dies suddenly. Faith requires a moment-by-moment inventory of our personal agendas and goals and a willingness to stop beating our proverbial donkey. Faith means taking action and traveling down the path all the while listening for God's prompting for what to say and do. It means recognizing God's working in our lives and not disregarding unexpected voices of truth.

We would be wise to learn from Balaam and be slower to criticize the trusted, reliable voices that question the direction we are heading. The reliable, dependable voices of wisdom in our lives are often the ones most willing to say what we do not want to hear. They make our journeys less burdensome as they carry some of the weight of life for us; they challenge us to stop and reflect on our journeys, sometimes in ways that are uncomfortable and disruptive to our personal preferences. They are the people who would rather see our foot crushed than our lives ruined; they can help us recognize God standing before us.

Our emotions can be important sources of information for us too. We face the challenge of approaching our emotional experience in a gentler way than Balaam approached his donkey. Our emotions can offer insight beyond the content of words and reason. Sometimes we need to create space for even unpleasant feelings and look to the parts of ourselves that we least want to listen to. Balaam's loyal donkey sees an obvious danger that Balaam cannot. When we are willing to find truth in the source of our frustration, we learn more about ourselves and about our path forward. God may be blocking our path to self-serving ends for good reason. To make sure Balaam gets the point, God asks him not to speak about anything until God tells him to speak. Before Balaam can honor what God asks him to do, he must confront the reality of how little he knows without God. Balaam says to Balak, "I have come to you now, but do I have power to say just anything? The word God puts in my mouth, that is what I must say" (Num. 22:38).

In the years following that first therapy group, I learned to listen to my feelings. I now have a wide vocabulary for my emotions, which I more freely express. I no longer feel fearful when emotions surface. I have developed the emotional intelligence to understand that tears are therapeutic and that our emotions help us, not harm us. In a moment of sadness, sharing tears with a friend can deepen our relationship. Distress can signal that some part of us needs attention and care. Sometimes we encounter our emotions in a way that does not feel at all like a positive spiritual experience of awareness. It can seem more like a frustration or roadblock, as it was for me in that first therapy group. Feelings can seem like unwanted visitors, but they need room to be present and expressed.

We would be wise to listen to the donkey and not to berate ourselves for our emotional realities. We can tune in, pay attention, and be mindful by listening everywhere for God's revelation, even in our own emotional experiences. Our emotions can seem crushing as they surface, but they impart important knowledge to us about ourselves. When we bring all of who we are to our faith, including our complex emotions, our faith can flow into our emotional lives and reveal God's presence in us.

Read Numbers 22:1-39. Ask yourself three questions: How do I see myself in this story? What is this story teaching me about myself? So what?

Prisons

About midnight Paul and Silas were praying and singing hymns to God, and the other prisoners were listening to them. Suddenly there was such a violent earthquake that the foundations of the prison were shaken. At once all the prison doors flew open, and everyone's chains came loose.

—Acts 16:25-26 (NIV)

After his retirement, my dad got involved with a prison ministry. He regularly visits inmates and offers kindness and a listening ear without questioning the nature of the crimes they have committed. My dad and others from his church deliver notes written in crayon from elementary-school-aged children that urge the prisoners to make better choices. He brings soap, toothbrushes, and cookies. Most importantly, he brings an attitude of love. My dad tells a story of one day when his friend intended to minister to a prisoner, and the prisoner ended up ministering to him. My dad's friend told the inmate that he had not had a meaningful conversation with his daughter in two years. The man urged him strongly to go home that day and call her. Somehow the man's perspective from within the prison gave clarity to the freedoms that we take for granted. The man's clarity led my dad's friend out of his own relational prison. He went home and called his daughter that day, which granted some breaths of fresh air to their strained relationship. He went to the prison that day thinking he was doing a favor for a prisoner, but the favor was done for him.

If we are willing to listen, we encounter voices of truth in unexpected places. The greatest sermons of our lives do not necessarily come from behind a pulpit. Moses encounters God in a burning bush, and Paul is blinded by a bright light that leads to his conversion on the road to Damascus. (See Exodus 3; Acts 9:1-20.) When Paul and Silas are accused of causing uproar in the city, they are flogged and jailed; from the jail cell they sing hymns and pray. (See Acts 16:16-25.) The prison walls cannot suppress the expression of their faith. Though they are not in a church, they continue to worship.

When we carry the attitude of being in constant worship, when we consider that everything in our life might be a church service with different types and styles of sermons from everyday people, we can begin hearing God's voice more often—even from within the walls of a prison. God is revealed to me most in everyday activities. I can hear the voice of God on Tuesday afternoons and Saturday nights just as well as Sunday mornings if I listen for it. There are no limits to where and through whom God can speak.

Recently, I sensed God speaking to me through the ending of a movie. God prompted me to remember that sometimes I am center stage, other times I am an important member of someone else's audience, and both roles are equally important. Another time, God spoke through my IHOP server. She laughed with deep understanding and great patience when my toddler wanted cereal, which was not on the menu. She could see the dilemma through my son's eyes. She spoke about how we throw adult versions of tantrums when we don't get what we want, yet we are puzzled by our children's feelings and preferences. Another time, God spoke through an insightful woman who cuts my hair as she told me about her clients. Some people come into the salon for a consultation requesting "something really different." Then they insist that they do not want to lose any length or change their hair color. Options for "something really different" become limited at that point. When we put too many limits on how and when we allow ourselves to hear from God, we have fewer options for spiritual growth and change.

We can open our senses to normal, everyday conversations and events. Truth from God can appear in nearly any form. Is God speaking to you through a conversation, a song, or a movie? Maybe God will challenge you to act on what you learn. Be open to it, and don't let your prisons contain you.

Read Acts 16:16-40. Ask yourself three questions: How do I see myself in this story? What is this story teaching me about myself? So what?

Fear

The fear of the Lord is instruction in wisdom.

—Proverbs 15:33

I know fear as a normal human emotion, one that can prompt a fight-or-flight response in the presence of a threat or perceived threat.[1] I know it as a personal experience and a vicarious experience. During college, I worked as a bank teller. One day during a shift, I took a lunch break and drove to a nearby restaurant. Within minutes of my returning, a masked man with a gun entered the bank. His intimidating and threatening presence struck fear in my heart. He slammed the gun on the counter in front of me and demanded that I hand over the money from my drawer. My hands shook as I opened the drawer and threw stacks of bills on the counter. I quickly ducked behind a wall along with the other three tellers. The man threatened to begin shooting and counted down from ten. During the moments we all were huddled together on the floor we believed he was about to kill us. I released a simultaneous string of cursing and desperate prayer. I wondered if my life was about to end. I listened intently. Time seemed to stand still, but soon I no longer heard the man's voice. The room was silent except for the slight whimpers of fear from my coworkers. We slowly rose from our corners of crouched desperation, and police officers arrived soon thereafter.

The robbery experience was a near miss for me. What if I had returned from my break just a little bit later, walked in, and surprised the thief? What if he had begun shooting? While he got the money, he was caught and arrested soon afterward. I am grateful that he left the bank when he did and we were all left physically unharmed.

Gavin de Becker is a specialist in assessing risk and threat for the CIA and other organizations. In his book *The Gift of Fear*,[2] he draws a sharp distinction between true fear and worry. While fear is a gift signaling the presence of danger, worry comes from our imagination or memory. De Becker writes that while true fear allows us to tune in to our environment and act accordingly, worry complicates and clutters the present moment and makes us less safe.

I understand the fear of God as similar to the true fear Gavin de Becker describes. The fear of God includes reverence and awe that can be best accessed when we are free of worry. When we can suspend worry, we can discern the quiet prompting of the Spirit working through us to give us direction. Then we can respond to the many cues in our environment. When we are free of worry, we are free to tune in deeply to all the opportunities God sets before us in what occurs around us. We are more likely to hear God in unlikely places. The Gospel writer Matthew emphasizes the uselessness of worry: "Can any of you by worrying add a single hour to your span of life?" (Matt. 6:27).

The fear of God helps us keep things in perspective. When we know our lives are in God's hands, we can quiet the speculation in our hearts about what might happen next and instead hear the wisdom we need for this moment. When we feel a pull to ruminate about the past or rehearse for the future, we are wise to bring ourselves back to the demands and joys of the present moment where we can have a healthy and true fear of God. We can set aside our worry and be ready to act on the internal prompting of the Spirit.

As mentioned in our reflection on *Kihaps* earlier this week, we can experience spiritual restoration through the practice of *lectio divina*, the sacred reading of scripture. Proverbs 15 is a great text for practicing *lectio divina*. As a reminder, the practice involves the following steps:

1. Read a passage of scripture slowly and contemplatively until one phrase stands out.
2. Rest on that phrase and write it down.
3. Prayerfully repeat it and listen for what God may be revealing to you through the scripture.

Begin by reading Proverbs 15 *slowly* and taking in each word and phrase. Stop when a word or phrase seems to hold particular meaning and relevance for you. The idea is not to move quickly through all of Proverbs 15 but to listen for God to reveal something to you through some portion of the scripture. This morning, verse 23 stood out to me: "To make an apt answer is a joy to anyone, and a word in season, how good it is!" I paused and wrote the verse in my journal. I closed my eyes and meditated on the words. I felt that God directed me to the passage as a reminder of how powerful a well-timed, loving response to another person can be. I recalled times others have responded or not responded to me in loving ways. I am approaching my day with greater awareness of how important my responses are to Dusty, my children, my clients, my friends, and others I encounter. I may not provide an apt answer to everyone I meet, but today I will be more aware of my responses to others.

Try *lectio divina* for yourself with Proverbs 15. Allow the practice to help you feel more focused, empowered, and intentional throughout the rest of the day. Be present, listen, and respond.

Read Proverbs 15. Ask yourself three questions: How do I see myself in this story? What is this story teaching me about myself? So what?

WEEKEND PRACTICE
Creating Sacred Spaces

This week we discovered God's truth in a monastery and a Taekwondo *dojang*. We considered that God's messages can come from many voices and places. We let go of worry and freed up attention to God's purposes in the moment. We made space for our emotions to see what they might be able to teach us about ourselves and about God.

This weekend, your challenge is to create a sacred space somewhere in your home or neighborhood. My everyday sacred space is my desk in the corner of my living room, my favorite room in our house. A large window allows the room to fill with light, especially in late afternoon. When I look out the window, I see birds, squirrels, chipmunks, and other animals scurrying around the front yard. The trees flower in an array of colors in the spring, become full and green in the summer, and transition through brilliant colors of fall into the more stark and cool brown of the brief Atlanta winter. I write, pray, and journal at this desk. The blue orchid on my desk absorbs light from the front window and offers a bit of life, color, and beauty in the space. It stands next to a framed photograph of my three sons. A couple of favorite books, including Stephen King's *On Writing*, are propped next to my printer. My Scotty's Brewhouse mug is filled with my favorite types of pens and markers and reminds me of Muncie, Indiana, where I lived for five years during graduate school. A canvas with six giraffes on it hangs above my desk. The giraffes in the picture stand tall and grounded, looking straight ahead, united and independently strong at the same time. The space is sacred because it is a place of comfort, prayer, creation, and purposeful work, and it is one of the few places in my home that is my own and not a shared space. It is a quiet place of comfort, focus, self-expression, and peace.

Whether your sacred space is a room in your house, a corner of a park, or a certain table in a coffee shop, you can claim it as your own. Choose a place that is free from unpleasant distractions where you can feel at peace. Let it become a place of prayer and a place of reevaluating how you are doing. Choose and go to the space at least one time this weekend. While you are there, try journaling about the following questions:

1. What does it mean to you to spend time in the dwelling place of God? How do you envision yourself as God's dwelling place?

2. What aspects of your life right now involve calm, relaxing moments? What aspects of your life involve powerful, effective moments? How do you feel about your current balance between the two?

3. When have you heard from God in an unlikely place? What did you sense that God was trying to say to you?

4. Who or what speaks with the donkey's voice that you don't want to listen to right now? What is this person or emotion telling you, and why don't you want to listen?

5. Where in your life do you experience worry that may be blocking your ability to hear from God? What steps can you take to let go of worry?

Silent Comfort

Now when Job's three friends heard of all these troubles that had come upon him, each of them set out from his home—Eliphaz the Temanite, Bildad the Shuhite, and Zophar the Naamathite. They met together to go and console and comfort him. When they saw him from a distance, they did not recognize him, and they raised their voices and wept aloud; they tore their robes and threw dust in the air upon their heads. They sat with him on the ground seven days and seven nights, and no one spoke a word to him, for they saw that his suffering was very great.

—Job 2:11-13

I remember my first therapy session with the therapist who would play the most central role in my emotional healing: I used my knowledge of psychology to diagnose myself, outline my presenting problems, and state my desired outcomes. I confidently estimated that a year of therapy would be ample time to explore, tweak, and generally fix my emotional struggles. As it turns out, my estimate was off by years, even though I was highly invested and offered consistent effort. Therapy is more of a process than an event; it often requires more time and effort than we expect as we work toward a sense of peace, resolution, and internal healing. Early in my therapy, my therapist said to me, "The psyche does not like to be rushed."[1] I made a mental note of the comment but determined that I would be the one outstanding client with an impressively efficient psyche. But she was absolutely right. The process was frustratingly slow. In hindsight, I would not trade away one minute of my therapy because slow healing also meant real healing without shortcuts. Restoring wholeness to a wounded heart does not happen with great efficiency.

For me, slow healing also meant many silences in my therapist's office. Some silences felt pressured and uncomfortable, while other silences healed deeply. The discomfort and pressure often came from my expectations that I move through therapy at a faster and more efficient pace. The healing silences took place when I could create space for my pain and allow my therapist to witness it and support me in it. She allowed me to sit with difficult emotions and questions without rushing to fix them or make them go away.

Restoring wholeness is a spiritual challenge. So many of our lives are affected by suffering from cancer, miscarriages or stillborn babies, house fires, poverty, suicide, abuse, homelessness, and addictions. These are only a few of the circumstances that leave wounded people in their wake with meager efforts to stay afloat and search for healing. We seek rational explanations, but too often injustice seems to trump what seems right and makes sense to us. We all are surrounded by pain, and we heal only when we find strategies for coping with it and responding to it.

Some of us cope by minimizing emotional pain or blaming the victims. Others distract ourselves with happier thoughts. Some of us check out and escape our pain as often as possible by using drugs or alcohol, shopping, eating, working, or exercising to numb ourselves. Others embrace the pain so fully that it becomes part of our identity. Still others feel a torturous blend of compassion and helplessness; we can fully acknowledge the harm that has been done to us, but we don't know where to begin in finding or facilitating healing. There are also those of us who take a giant step away from emotion into a rigidly cognitive sphere and attempt to explain our pain from a distant, philosophical place. We apply rules to our pain and interpret reasons for it. Others slap trite, oversimplified phrases onto heartache like a smiley-faced sticker. Some of us fully feel the brunt of our pain and work through it. Most of us engage in all the above strategies at one time or another.

The story of Job recounts some of the worst pain anyone has ever endured as well as human efforts to explain it. Job encounters several types of responses. We are told Job is righteous and doing quite well in life until God and Satan start conversing about him. Satan observes Job's faithfulness, but asserts that his faith and praise stems only from his good fortune and blessing. Satan challenges God with the notion that if Job endures hardship, he will curse God. God listens to

Satan's argument but persists in his confidence in Job's faith. So God gives Satan the OK to inflict every type of pain on Job if he spares Job's life. (See Job 1:1-12.)

The first wave of tragedy strikes: In less than twenty-four hours, Job receives word that he has lost his livestock, servants, and ten children. Then he endures sores over his entire body and suffers such physical pain that his wife encourages him to go ahead and curse God. Job refuses. When Job's friends Eliphaz, Bildad, and Zophar approach him, Job is so steeped in pain that he is unrecognizable. (See Job 1:13–2:12.)

The friends' shining moment happens early in the story as Job's pain is first unfolding. They approach him and weep, validating the intensity of Job's suffering, and then sit with him in silence for seven days. His friends are at their best before they start to interpret Job's pain when they sit with him and do not say anything. They are silent but present in his pain.

But then Job's friends step in to intervene and try their hand at interpreting existential suffering and tragedy. When they open their mouths, things go downhill rather quickly. After Job reaches such depth of pain that he curses the day of his own birth, Eliphaz assumes Job has done something wrong to deserve painful circumstances, and he tells Job so. Eliphaz goes on to preach to Job about how good God is. Bildad suggests Job just needs to repent to God. Zophar chimes in that Job is babbling and that he is guilty of wrongdoing and deserves punishment. These strategies are less than supportive. However, amid his terrible circumstances, Job persists in faithfulness. He reflects. He questions his circumstances. He shows impatience and frustration with God. (See Job 3.) At some point in our lives, we all share in Job's dialogue.

Our efforts to support others change and evolve. Sometimes we get it wrong, and other times we get it right. When we get it wrong, it's important to stay engaged and keep trying to get it right rather than disengage and give up. Regardless of why we believe pain occurs, we all face the challenge of acknowledging that pain exists and that our loving presence with the person suffering does more than our efforts to explain it. We often do much more to support the people we love by offering our silent presence rather than trying to explain events that are beyond human understanding. Offering a silent presence can mean stopping by, sitting with someone, and listening. It often means resisting the urge to explain why our loved one is in inexplicable pain. A hug and an attentive ear can do so much more to help the healing process.

We can come alongside one another and recognize that there may be pain that has no biblical, theological explanation. Instead of offering one, we can simply be present with one another. We can remember and acknowledge that our pain is not all of who we are. Pain does not have to encompass and define us. Whether or not your loved ones show and voice their pain, it is there. We can follow the early example of Job's friends and be willing to listen quietly. We can give our loved ones and ourselves time, patience, and loving acceptance. We may need more than seven days, and many of us do not respond well to being pushed to talk before we are ready. Our healing paths often are long, and there is pain that lasts a lifetime. Allow others—allow yourself—to wrestle with tough questions and move through the process at a manageable pace. We can all move through our pain with more comfort in each other's silent, supportive presence.

Read Job 2:1-3:26. If time allows, read Job 2:1–14:22, or even the whole book of Job. Ask yourself three questions: How do I see myself in this story? What is this story teaching me about myself? So what?

As Yourself

[Jesus said to the lawyer], *"'You shall love the Lord your God with*
all your heart, and with all your soul, and with all your mind.'
This is the greatest and first commandment. And a second is like
it: 'You shall love your neighbor as yourself.'"

—Matthew 22:37-39

A few years ago, I attended my twentieth high school reunion after making the nine-hour drive from Atlanta, Georgia, back to central Illinois with Dusty. We arrived just in time for him to drop me off at the high school so I could jump onto the homecoming parade float labeled, "Mahomet-Seymour Class of '95."

I rode through the streets of my small hometown waving to my kindergarten teacher, former neighbors, and classmates. Some I embraced immediately. I've kept in touch with a handful of my best friends in Illinois. Some people were hard to recognize at first, but within a minute of conversing with them, I'd notice familiar mannerisms and recognition would set in. One of my closest friends sat next to me on the float and leaned over occasionally to whisper names under her breath. I deeply appreciated her tutorial on who was who. I saw classmates from other graduating classes, and some from my own. Memories of French class, my basketball team, Friday night football games, lockers, and life in high school came flooding back. When our float approached Main Street in the center of town, Dusty waved to me from the side of the street and hopped on the float with all of us. I thanked God for my recent years with him in Atlanta and for my history in Mahomet, Illinois. We rode down Main Street in perfect fall weather while the sun shone warmly on our faces.

I was on a high from reconnecting with old friends. I saw my Driver's Ed teacher at the homecoming football game. I took a tour of the high school, some of which looks exactly the same. I noted with both regret and amusement the place I'd gotten reprimanded for asking a friend to fix my car so my parents wouldn't find out about a dent. I saw the place where my locker had been and the library with many fewer books where I'd spent detention for forging a pass to get myself out of study hall. I found my assigned seats in the calculus and physics room and the stop sign I ran over after failing to scrape ice adequately from my windshield one December morning. I walked around the football field, where I'd spent hours talking and laughing with friends. I heard the marching band play. Back in the band room, I asked the teens in the color guard if I could toss someone's flag and rifle. My muscle memory kicked in and both motions came back to me in an instant. I caught the flag and then the rifle effortlessly. I saw the new field house where it would have been nice to have played basketball. I sat in the auditorium seats remembering my role as Aunt Eller in *Oklahoma!* in 1995, the year of the Oklahoma City bombing.

As Dusty and I made the long drive back home to Atlanta, my mind raced through everything that had happened that weekend and everything that had happened over twenty years ago. I think my former classmates and I all walked around the reunion carrying our inner teenagers with us. I remembered the person I was, and I compared her to the person I am now. Sometimes I've wanted to forget who I was as a teenager, or at least some of the things I did. I have said countless prayers of gratitude that the world of social media was nonexistent during my teenage years. I am glad that snapshots of parties I attended in high school and college are not floating around in the cloud. I've now spent two decades trying to understand my earlier self, sometimes wanting to disown her, but ultimately trying to embrace her. I have had to acknowledge and understand that she—I—was doing the best that I could, as I believe we all were.

We all find our own ways of coping with life; but underneath appearances and behaviors, I believe we all hold in common many similar and important things. We've all tried on various identities. Maybe we have tried different cities, different colleges, different career paths, different religions, different marriages or relationships. We've asked spiritual questions, sought achievements, and embraced or avoided relationships with varying degrees of heartache. We've navigated difficult choices about what to carry on from our families of origin and what to leave behind. Most of us could do better than we are doing, but somehow we all are doing the best we can.

We all have to move toward a point of embracing and accepting ourselves in order to truly love other people. When a lawyer approaches Jesus to ask him which commandment is the greatest, Jesus responds, " 'You shall love the Lord your God with all your heart, and with all your soul, and with all your mind.' This is the greatest and first commandment. And a second is like it: 'You shall love your neighbor as yourself.' " *As yourself,* he says. Loving our neighbors as ourselves implies that we love ourselves. Jesus does not say to love our neighbors before or instead of ourselves but rather to love our neighbors *as* ourselves.

We open the door to loving others when we first come to terms with loving ourselves. Catholic priest Henri Nouwen points to the example of Jesus' cyclic progression of activity over the course of a day as recorded in the sixth chapter of Luke's Gospel.[1] During the night, Jesus retreats in prayer and solitude. In the morning, he moves to connection with his disciples. Then in the afternoon, he ministers. Jesus follows an unfolding rhythm of solitude, community, and ministry. If we hit the ground running, ministering to others before taking time for solitude, we will likely be depleted and frustrated soon afterward. God knows that our most effective work springs from love for ourselves and our communities following Jesus' model. When we embrace the love and energy God offers to us through prayerful solitude, we can find peace in God and approach community with greater confidence. When we can allow solitude, we can allow honest self-reflection. We can strip away our pretenses and our need to impress and find that God loves and embraces us as we are. It is best to start off *as yourself.* Then, we can emerge into the meaningful experience of community that God desires for us. By connecting first with the source of our identity in God, we allow love to flow first from our hearts into the lives of our close, trusted companions. Then the streams of our passions and capacity to give can extend into the larger community.

Solitude creates space for us to reflect on the challenge to love ourselves in the presence of God, where we can also know the truth about ourselves. The truth is that we are deeply loved, regardless of our choices and our worst moments. Reflecting on my high school years required me to forgive myself for my insecurities, my unhealthy attempts at relationships, and my unwise choices. I needed the path of therapy and spiritual growth that occurred between my high school years and my twenty-year reunion in order to return to my hometown with a different, more loving attitude toward myself. Loving myself as myself now frees me to love other people better than I used to. As I continue to move through the cycle of solitude in God's presence, time with trusted companions, and giving to the larger community, I will know and love myself as my neighbors and love my neighbors as myself. It's an interchangeable call to love; when we get better at doing one, we get better at doing the other.

Read Matthew 22:23-40. Ask yourself three questions: How do I see myself in this story? What is this story teaching me about myself? So what?

Snapping the Bowstrings

Delilah said to Samson, "Please tell me what makes your strength so great, and how you could be bound, so that one could subdue you."

—Judges 16:6

When I reflect on the dating relationships of my high school and college years, I am aware of some shared characteristics of the people I dated. There are times when I've failed to trust Dusty, not because he is untrustworthy but because others proved themselves untrustworthy. Likewise, there are times when he has assumed negative intentions on my part because others in his life have had negative intentions. Some of our negative reactions to others have more to do with our past relationships than with our current relationships.

One psychological theory posits that we are drawn to relationships that mimic the negative traits of those who raised us, those who most shaped our personalities.[1] We unconsciously seek out partners and deep friendships that hit the repeat button on the most painful dynamics in our lives. We focus intently on the ways that our significant other differs from those who have hurt us. In some ways, they differ greatly, but the unfolding of time and struggle reveals strikingly familiar dynamics. At the same time, our partners in love are drawn to us for their own reasons, to work out their own unresolved hurt, anger, and unfinished business. The closer we become to our partners, the more apparent the dynamics become. We notice that we are suddenly as angry with a spouse as we once were with a parent or family member. In the emotional intensity of a single moment, we catapult back into the shoes of our child or adolescent selves, or maybe both.

We may seek to make things right. Counseling, heart-to-heart talks, and shared life experiences may help us stay afloat amid the repetitive dynamics. We can seek to become self-aware of our baggage enough to see the patterns from across our lives and realize what we need from one another to heal. Most of us need help to reach that level of self-awareness. A psychologist I deeply respect once said that awareness leads to both acceptance and change. When I can understand that the invalidation I feel with my spouse is as much about a series of past relationships as it is about the current interaction, I make progress and begin to heal. I can choose to react differently in the moment and stop holding so much resentment against my spouse.

Therapy is a good place to further the process of self-awareness. We first need to know who we are, beloved children of God. In yesterday's reflection, we explored the importance of prioritizing solitude before relationships in the community. If we do not know we are the beloved children of God, we're going to expect someone in the community to make us feel special and worthy. Ultimately, another person cannot satisfy the need we have for the perfect, unconditional love of God.

When we come face-to-face with ourselves in a mirror that reflects what is true rather than just a cloudy approximation of the truth, we are freed to become people who can really give to others, really be unselfish, and release the impossible web of needs and expectations that we have been thrusting onto others. Other people are human. They are limited in their abilities to meet our needs, so we head down a frustrating path of disappointment when they are our sole source of life.

I've seen two major spiritual problems that can occur in relationships. The first occurs when we expect other people to be God to us, fulfilling all our needs and desires. The book of Judges includes the story of Samson. An angel foretells Samson's birth. Samson is known throughout his life for his incredible physical strength and his ability to take on and conquer as many as a thousand men. He is also a bit of a loose cannon: In one evening, he hires a prostitute and tears apart the city gates. Samson is clearly somewhat impulsive in his relationships with women, but he falls in love when he meets Delilah. However, she does not return his love. In fact, she is rather quick to betray him and hand him over to the Philistines for a handful of silver. The Philistines hate Samson because he has defeated many of their people in battle, single-handedly at times. Delilah, brazen and obvious in her attempts to locate his weakness, takes advantage of Samson. The Philistines want to kill him in revenge, and she collaborates fully with them in the pursuit of bringing him down.

In an intimate moment of vulnerability, Delilah asks Samson for the secret to his strength. This is a relational red flag, and Samson knows it on some level because he lies the first three times she asks the question. Each time, she attempts to capture him through the vulnerability he discloses. The first time, he says if he were tied in bowstrings he could be overcome. But when she tries it, he snaps the bowstrings. He must know immediately that she has betrayed him, that she is seeking his vulnerability and attempting to subdue him.

Samson's long, flowing locks of hair are the secret to his strength. Were his hair to be cut, he would be rendered physically powerless. Samson doesn't share this secret until the fourth time Delilah pleads with him. I imagine Samson feels some hesitation, but he stays with her despite her first three attempts to have him captured. The fourth time, he caves. He is tired and worn down from her persistence. So, sure enough, he is captured by the Philistines and put in jail. I wonder why he stays with Delilah after the first time she tries to facilitate his capture.

We easily see the problems when we read the story of Samson and Delilah, but we can overlook the same type of behavior in ourselves. We tend to do the same thing Samson did to some degree. We are drawn again and again to the same person to meet needs that they are unable or unwilling to meet, and each time this relationship results in problems for us. We end up in despair, rejection, and pain. Because of our love or infatuation with another, we cannot heed reason, self-protection, and wisdom. When we snap the bowstrings and realize what's happening, we make poor choices to stay involved instead of taking a healthy step back and moving on.

We unconsciously seek out people who are like those who have hurt us in the past to try to work through the relational dynamic and find healing. Without awareness, we are easy prey for relational predators. They are unfortunately everywhere. Some sit in positions of power, some are family members, and some are online. Some seem so captivating at first that we defy reason in our attempts to make it work with them despite all kinds of obvious warning signs. We need solitude, reflection, distance, and sometimes professional therapy to help us gain awareness of the harmful relational dynamic. We need the initiative to go to God for the needs that only God can meet. Only when Samson is in jail and removed from his toxic relationship with Delilah do his hair and his strength begin to grow back.

Sometimes my clients need time and distance away from a parent or other significant person in their lives as they sort through the many layers of what contributes to their struggle with anxiety, eating, or depression. Psychologists commonly urge clients not to "shop for milk at a hardware store."[2] We need to go to the grocery store for milk because that is where we can get milk. If we continue going to the hardware store looking for milk, we will only continue to get nails. Often we seek for our needs to be met in people who are unwilling or unable to support us fully.

The second problem occurs for those of us who try to be God to others rather than pointing those around us to God as the perfect and unconditional source of love, able to meet all needs. Other peoples' needs are great. If we open ourselves to the role of helper, we are wise to set some self-protective boundaries around our time and availability. We can acknowledge that we have limits to helping others. We can offer our hand, but the other must receive it. An unbalanced and overworked therapist or helper cannot sustain nourishment for others. When the helper takes time for self-compassion, reflection, and rejuvenation, people in the helper's life benefit too.

Trying to be God to others is a path to inevitable resentment and burnout. Realizing and setting our own limits can be freeing and enable us to do more effective counseling, ministry, and service for those around us. As a therapist, I cannot teach self-care or self-compassion if I do not practice setting my own limits. Sometimes it is the most loving thing to encourage another adult to take responsibility for his or her own circumstances, feelings, and preferences. I can be most helpful to my clients by discouraging their dependency on me. Whether we find ourselves in the role of a therapist, coach, friend, or concerned family member, we can empathize with someone's dilemma and ask, "What will you do about it?" rather than seeking to be the fixer and savior. Sometimes I have believed that if I worked hard enough as a therapist I could guarantee that a client would change. Not so. Instead I end up encouraging clients' dependency on me, and their default coping strategy becomes looking to me instead of using my support to build resources within themselves. Sometimes helping means letting go, refusing to be pulled into a dynamic that diminishes and disempowers another's sense of responsibility.

In the end, Samson's foolishness brings him down—and everyone around him as well. He regains strength as his hair grows back only to use it in one last act of revenge. Samson heaves his strength into the pillars supporting the center of the room where three thousand gather to make a spectacle of Samson. I wonder if Samson collapses the building on himself and the three thousand out of sheer resentment toward Delilah, out of shame that he has let himself be manipulated into capture, or out of anger at the Philistines for mocking his strength. Maybe it is all three.

Our relationships do not have to end like Samson's did, under the collapse of anger, shame, and resentment. I cannot think of anything that is so dependent or so narcissistic as to adopt one of these two beliefs about our relationships with other individuals. When we make a deity of ourselves or others, we miss out on greater confidence and trust that is available in God. By spending time in solitude to gain self-awareness, we create the capacity for healthier relationships, and everyone we love benefits. We can prevent the escalation of repetitive, destructive family dynamics. We can stop shopping for milk at a hardware store. We can look for opportunities to follow Jesus' example and return to solitude. We can connect with God in prayer by bringing our burdens, sitting in silence, and listening for God's voice.

Read Judges 16:4-31. Ask yourself three questions: How do I see myself in this story? What is this story teaching me about myself? So what?

The Collective She

> *If the whole body were an eye, where would the sense of hearing be? If the whole body were an ear, where would the sense of smell be? But in fact God has placed the parts in the body, every one of them, just as he wanted them to be. If they were all one part, where would the body be? As it is, there are many parts, but one body.*
>
> —1 Corinthians 12:17-19 (NIV)

At one of my Taekwondo black belt tests, I executed a knife-hand strike with my right hand in an attempt to break a thick board. A knife-hand strike involves making a flat, open hand with fingers held tightly together and the thumb tightly tucked in to support the edge of the hand. The strike begins with one arm extended and is delivered in a slicing motion with the palm upward. The goal is to break a board with the side of the hand while making the swift, strong slicing motion. During each of my belt tests, I am challenged to try something I've never done before for the board-breaking section of the test. I can choose a different technique, my left or right hand or foot, or a greater number or thickness of boards to break. In this test, I had to demonstrate three different board breaks, and I tried the knife-hand strike first.

Sometimes with board breaks, I am not one hundred percent sure I can do it; but I try anyway. I felt some trepidation as I looked at the board and, sure enough, I failed to break it multiple times. My hand slammed into the solid

88

board, and I felt a shot of pain extend up my arm. It often hurts little or not at all when a board breaks, but pain comes when a board does not break. My confidence waned with each attempt, and my hand really started to hurt. Eventually, I tried the breaking technique with two thinner boards stacked together rather than the thicker one, and I broke them on the first try. After the test, our Master called the black belts to himself for an instructional moment. He talked about how a hand technique does not just involve the hand, and that we shouldn't even think of a knife-hand strike as a hand technique. He explained that we use our whole bodies when we break boards. The hand just happens to be the point of the body that makes contact with the board.

Despite many divisions, perspectives, political stances, and denominational structures, we are one body as believers in Christ. As Christians, we look to biblical standards of excellence to help create order and a sense of what behaviors are appropriate and honorable. Proverbs 31:10-31 has often been cited as an ideal to which Christian women should aspire. The passage describes a virtuous woman and provides a description of characteristics that no one woman could possibly attain in full. An understandable takeaway from reading Proverbs 31:10-31 is, "How am I, or anyone, supposed to accomplish all of that in one lifetime?" The woman described in this passage transcends mere beauty and charm, and everyone in the house loves her. She wakes up early *and* stays up late. Working and managing a household, she buys, sells, trades, sews, plants, cooks, and manages a group of laborers. She has toned arms *and* makes time to give to those in poverty. She creates her own clothing line, and everyone in her home wears it. In her downtime, she makes bedding. While she's sharing all her wisdom and teachings, everyone still loves her, which seems to suggest a genuineness and complete lack of narcissism in her. Somehow amid all the toil, she is tuned in to what's going on at home and finds the carefree ability to laugh at what's to come. She manages to wear strength like a sundress and dignity like a flowing tunic.

I wonder whether we would do better to understand this passage as a non-gender-specific call to all of us to be as a unified whole, a group of interdependent parts of a body of believers who each offer a unique contribution of nobility and virtue, rather than through the Western, Americanized lens that highlights the pursuit of individual excellence. Other passages in the Bible support the idea that God gives us unique gifts, and that none of us alone is self-sufficient. We depend on Christ to fuel the energy behind the whole system as we each play a uniquely valuable role within it. The body of Christ refers to the family of Christian believers, interdependent and functioning communally rather than individually. A spiritual body of believers can benefit from viewing Proverbs

31:10-31 as a shared goal. Maybe each *she* in the passage is a different she. Maybe some of the *she*s are even *he*s. The whole body breaks a board, not just one hand. If we could view Proverbs 31 as an interdependent, communal goal rather than an individual goal, its accolades may seem not only more doable but also more unifying. As an individual ideal, the description sets a high bar against which all women measure themselves and lends itself to comparisons among women. Such spiritual comparisons are a fruitless use of our energy.

We, as a body of believers, have the most potential impact in transcending an obstacle by approaching it in the same way. When we join in a communally shared set of beliefs and values, we have the most impact not by highlighting our own individual contributions to breaking through obstacles but by working together as a spiritual body and supporting one another's strengths. The pastor happens to be the one preaching. The parents happen to be the ones nurturing, providing, and loving their children. The Bible study leader facilitates and handles logistics, while the study participants add valuable perspectives through their own lenses that highlight various pieces of a complex, shared truth. Each person illuminates a corner in someone else's shadowed understanding of God.

There is beauty in being part of a spiritual body of believers. When we do community well, our identity as a body with many parts frees us of a need to compare ourselves to one another. If we can unify, we can celebrate one another's contributions to our overall goals. Some of us can get up early, and others can stay up late. Some can cook, clean, sew or be tuned in to what's going on at home and at school, while others can trade, buy, sell, or create. The creative woman can appreciate the early riser, and the night owl can appreciate the buyer. The buyer can respect the seller, and the one who is tuned in at church or school can share insight with the others. The practical person and the fun person can learn from one another. Together we can break through an obstacle without trying to be the lone hand, doing all the work by itself, and slamming into an obstacle it cannot break without the support of the whole body. As you read the description of the ideal woman in Proverbs 31, consider taking a personal spiritual inventory. Which *one* challenge may be your contribution to the overall movement of the body?

Read Proverbs 31:10-31. Ask yourself three questions: How do I see myself in this story? What is this story teaching me about myself? So what?

Stones and Dust

Jesus bent down and wrote with his finger on the ground. When they kept on questioning him, he straightened up and said to them, "Let anyone among you who is without sin be the first to throw a stone at her." And once again he bent down and wrote on the ground.

—John 8:6-8

I had no idea what I was getting into as parent council president of our church preschool. One of my responsibilities as president was to oversee the preschool's consignment sale. The sale is a major undertaking. In the past, I'd shown up the morning of the sale, browsed, and bought a few items. My new role opened my eyes to an enormous system at work behind the scenes with many complex moving parts. The sale's cochairs coordinate volunteers for several shifts over a three-day sale, negotiate the church space that will be used, tag donated items, organize the drop-off and shelving of thousands of items, communicate with consignors, advertise the sale, and determine where the leftover donated items will go. The cash registers, credit card machines, and data have to be tracked. Disgruntled people need calls back. Parents in red aprons guard big-ticket strollers, play sets, and name-brand clothing. The security has to be top-notch, as people wandering through during set-up day have been caught red-handed trying to lift items from the sale or stash them in hiding places to reserve for themselves. One woman was caught trying to hide shoes in the bathroom and was left to the mercy of her accusers. It could become easy in that moment, after hours of volunteer work, to unfurl judgment on the shoe-stasher.

In the Gospel of John, a woman is caught in a different act, and Jesus responds in an unexpected way. He addresses and challenges her accusers rather than directing judgment at her. Caught in the act of adultery, the woman may already be stirring in shame, hurling stones at herself. Or she may not feel any remorse. There is no disputing that she's broken the law and sinned, and the crowd is ready and waiting to point the finger at her and carry out her sentence. The law says she should be stoned for the offense, and the Pharisees ask Jesus to respond to the situation. (See John 7:53–8:5.)

Jesus, however, does not point his finger at the woman or at her accusers but instead into the dirt. We know he writes something, but the Gospel writer does not disclose what he writes. Perhaps the content of his writing is not as important as the simple fact that he draws attention to the dust of the earth in a moment of human accusation and condemnation. Maybe he points to the dust as a subtle reminder that "all go to one place; all are from the dust, and all turn to dust again" (Eccles. 3:20). As human beings turn on one another, he reminds them of what we all share: We are all human, and that implies shared struggle.

In pointing to the dust, Jesus also points to the origin of life. From dust, God has formed human beings. (See Genesis 2:7.) From the commonness of dust arises the complexity and mystery of human life. As we acknowledge our shared humanity, we let go of the illusion that we are more or less valuable than other people. Our identity as dust can help us to be mindful of our place in relation to God and mindful of the capacity for life. We can rest in the comforting truth that we are dust, knowing that it is God who breathes life into us. We can stop categorizing, labeling, and trying to decide who is most and least saved. Such an acknowledgment transforms us and allows us to realize our full potential and be filled with the life God intends. Each person is complex, surprising, and full of potential for change and growth. But first, we have to acknowledge the dust.

When Jesus challenges the crowd by asking that the first one to throw a stone be someone who has not sinned at all, the crowd disperses, and the woman is left with no accusers. Jesus does not say that anyone in the crowd who has not committed adultery should throw the first stone but anyone who has not sinned at all. They, and we, can be quick to see faults in others and overlook or justify our own. We are quick to spotlight and magnify the wretchedness of the sins we happen not to commit. In this poignant moment, Jesus levels our pious comparisons and refuses to rank the seriousness of different types of sins. When he speaks, Jesus very clearly says to her that since no one around her can condemn her, he does not condemn her either. Not one of her accusers can claim a sin-less life. Being addressed and challenged by Jesus seems to give them a differ-ent, more merciful perspective. Jesus can claim a sinless life. (See 2 Corinthians 5:21.) If anyone were in a place to assess someone else's choices, it would be him. Yet, he does not condemn the woman. He does not enter into a conversation of ruminating and stirring over what she has done. What a different world we would live in if we lived out Jesus' attitude of love and forgiveness in this passage.

Jesus consistently challenges those who are quick to accuse: "First take the log out of your own eye, and then you will see clearly to take the speck out of your neighbor's eye" (Matt. 7:5). Self-reflection is foundational to a life of faith. Self-reflection involves ongoing assessment and adjustments. After years of what I considered a pretty complete self-analysis in the personal therapy of my late twenties and early thirties, I was consistently in a better place emotionally. I felt better about myself and more grounded than ever before. I made time for what mattered to me while offering energy to help others. I continued to work on my own sense of personal growth and balance, but I had found a general rhythm of self-care and giving that felt good to me; so eventually my therapy sessions became few and far between. Then when I was thirty-eight, I had a particularly challenging year. I felt too much pressure to care for everyone around me, had too little down time for myself, and felt the weight of some important deci-sions for my children. A familiar dark cloud of depression settled in on me as I had an increasingly hard time locating a sense of self-worth. I became my own accuser. While I could still acknowledge and celebrate a solid recovery from eating disorder episodes for over fifteen years, the associated perfectionism and nagging self-doubt resurfaced. I doubted my ability to parent despite caring for three thriving children. I doubted my knowledge and expertise in doing therapy despite positive connections with clients who were progressing. The emotional pain of my earlier struggles felt present again in my self-criticism, so I began to see my therapist more often. She reminded me that I was believing negative things about myself that simply weren't true. I rediscovered my more compas-sionate, empathic internal voice and got back on course much more quickly than I had in the past after identifying my familiar vulnerabilities.

Though we do not know whether the woman in this story felt shame, guilt, or other self-condemning emotions, we all have experienced such metaphorical stones. Sometimes the stones of self-condemnation are weighty, more like boul-ders. Some stones represent a regretful burst of anger, an unspoken but growing resentment, or a failed marriage. Other times they are quiet but persistently nagging internal insistences that we wrap a perfect present or get an A+ on an exam, or achieve a particular look through a new fashion, workout, or eating plan. Jesus' response invites us to an added challenge to drop the stones we hurl at ourselves. When our conscience nudges us in our less-than-holy moments, we can release the weights we carry on our own shoulders by dropping our stones of self-condemnation.

When I self-reflect and become more empathic with myself, I can extend greater empathy toward others and drop stones of accusation, just as the woman's accusers did. When they reflected on their own lives, they could release their blame on her. Jesus' decision not to condemn the woman does not depend on her repentance. We do not know whether she repents or feels one iota of regret for her adulterous escapade. Even when caught in the act, many go on to deny their offenses within themselves and to others. Nevertheless, Jesus does not condemn. He urges her to go, to keep living, to keep moving forward. He also urges her not to sin again. Jesus knows it is in her best interest to take a different path forward, but his forgiveness is not contingent on it. I suspect that in light of the Son of God coming to her defense amid a guilty verdict, she is moved to do something honorable with her second chance. But in reality, we write the ending to that story with our own lives.

When we witness other people judging and condemning, we can respond as Jesus did by boldly and lovingly pointing to our shared humanity and urging them to drop the stones. We can urge accusers to self-examine, and we can do some self-reflection as well. We can ask those caught in painful choices and consequences to make different choices. When confronted with the unwise decisions of another, we can drop the stones and release the people around us from our condemnation. We can be the voice that both defends and challenges them. Though we may not share the struggle of the person next to us, we share the experience of struggling in some way with some persistent thorn that presents itself again and again in our own life. In Jesus, God becomes fully human, fully relatable to us. So when we are caught in the act of sin, by others or by ourselves, we can go to God knowing that Jesus urges us to move forward. We can self-reflect and know that better choices will inevitably have better outcomes. Little by little, we become more like Christ—less accusing and more loving to ourselves and others.

Read John 8:2-11. Ask yourself three questions: How do I see myself in this story? What is this story teaching me about myself? So what?

WEEKEND PRACTICE

Forgiving

This week we considered the love and compassion that can flow between us in relationships when we connect with Jesus. We reflected on Job's trials and the silent comfort of his friends. We considered loving yourself as well as your neighbor. We read Samson's story and learned from his repetitive unsuccessful attempts to be in a mutually loving relationship with Delilah. We considered the whole body of believers to be part of the *she* in Proverbs 31. And we revisited Jesus' unconditional compassion and love in the story of the woman caught in adultery, while learning to challenge accusers and ourselves to self-reflect.

This weekend's practice focuses on forgiveness. Forgiveness is essential if love and compassion are to flow freely between people in relationships. Instead of approaching forgiveness as a series of events, we will try approaching it as a way of life.[1] Forgiveness fully acknowledges the harm that's been done but does not require forgetting or minimizing an offense. Forgiveness is a choice to no longer punish ourselves or others for harm or hurt from the past. Forgiving someone lets *us* off the hook by releasing our burden of anger, resentment, and emotional pain. Forgiving someone does not mean that we must confront or reconcile with that person. Reconciliation requires two people, but forgiveness can be done as an individual practice.

Consider the grievances and grudges you currently hold within your heart. List them, but don't expect yourself to complete the process of forgiving all of the offenses in one weekend. Forgiveness is a difficult practice, and it's essential that we start from a doable place. When we learn a new sport, instrument, or skill, we start with the fundamentals and build on them gradually. We can do the same with forgiving. Choose two offenses that feel doable to tackle in a prayerful, focused weekend, and write them down. Start with offenses that do not stem from your deepest hurts and longings. Choose one offense that requires forgiving yourself, and one offense that requires forgiving another person.

Identify a forgiveness statement for each of the offenses. Be mindful that forgiveness is more of a choice than an emotion. Fully acknowledge the pain, annoyance, and hurt involved, but also make the choice to let go of it.

Here are two example situations and forgiveness statements:

1. If I choose to forgive my husband for leaving dirty dishes in the sink, I may say, "I am choosing to forgive my husband. Dirty dishes in the sink are annoying and inconvenient. By forgiving I am choosing not to punish my husband for leaving the dishes." Or, "I am remembering my husband is human, just like me. I've left dirty dishes in the sink too, and I am choosing to drop my stone of accusation."

2. If I choose to forgive myself for taking on too many responsibilities, I may say, "I have not set the limits I want to set, but I am choosing to drop this stone of accusation and let go of my frustration toward myself. I can move forward making different choices."

Write your own statements below or in your journal:

1.

2.

Throughout this weekend, when each of the offenses comes to mind, say the statement to yourself. In doing so, you are practicing a new way of thinking about the offense. If you choose to, you can take an additional step that will serve as a symbol of letting go of the offense. Write each of the offenses on a stone, and then throw the stones into a lake or stream as you say the statement of forgiveness. You can do this by yourself or with a trusted friend or group of friends. The stones will still exist, and they will be there in your memory, but you will have chosen to release them. You will stop giving them power to weigh you down. At the end of the weekend, journal about any progress you have experienced on your path to forgiving the two offenses.

WEEK FIVE: WHY YOUR FAITH NEEDS FUN

Go, eat your bread with enjoyment, and drink your wine with a
merry heart; for God has long ago approved what you do.
—Ecclesiastes 9:7

For most of my life, I had my share of fun and creative play. As a child, I created plays and magic shows with my sister. I pretended to be Sandy in *Grease,* transforming from nerdy to cool through song. Other days I was a character from *The Dukes of Hazaard,* jumping in and out of a parked car window and running from the law. During high school, I loved basketball, color guard, and every musical group I could join. I played exciting roles in the school musicals and had fun with my friends almost every day. During college, I played intramural ice hockey. I got an eyebrow ring. I sang in a women's choir. With my friends, I played broomball, a hilarious version of hockey involving a ball, a stick with a triangular base, and sneakers instead of ice skates. Our competitive personalities shined, and we laughed until we peed. We watched Stephen King's *The Shining* and freaked ourselves out. We decided on a *Grease* marathon late one night and still got through the week. I started my practice of Taekwondo, and I discovered my love for psychology.

During my late twenties, work became a central focus for me. I had achieved my long-term, hard-earned goal of becoming a psychologist. I'd spent ten years measuring time and progress in terms of semesters and syllabi. It happened slowly, but during graduate school, most of my passions got rescheduled, postponed, and pushed to a lesser priority. I lost touch with many of my close friends. I spent most of my time studying or talking with classmates about "the program" over cheap beer while our spouses talked among themselves. I ran a couple of races and enjoyed time with my classmates, but most of my down time occurred within a cloud of stress with every major project, exam, and requirement looming ahead of me. My efforts were graded and evaluated microscopically all the way until graduation day.

After graduation, I experienced a type of quarter-life crisis. I wondered what to do next, now that I was free of the semester-based life. There were no more grades. Though there was a degree of evaluation in my work from supervisors, they trusted me more than they evaluated me. I was not prepared for the indecision that would surface and the longing to reconnect with my earlier passions.

The writer of Ecclesiastes, generically addressed as "The Teacher," describes the "unhappy business" of accumulating knowledge and wisdom. (See Ecclesiastes 1:13.) While wisdom and knowledge have value, there is more to life. God points us toward the importance of work and play. The Teacher writes that many life events are meaningless, "chasing after the wind" (Eccles. 1:14). The Teacher acquires great wealth but sees emptiness in it. He points instead to the enduring worth of enjoying eating, drinking, and engaging in fulfilling work. (See Ecclesiastes 2:24.)

As one who has overindulged in both eating and drinking, I feel guarded as I approach this passage. Could eating quality food and drinking wine really be two of the most valuable parts of life? In my experience, yes! But could God really be okay with that? When done mindfully and joyfully, and not out of compulsion, numbing, or a need to escape and distract, eating and drinking are two truly great and God-approved gifts. I would love to see our culture embrace mindful eating and drinking as spiritual steps forward, rather than condemning them as overindulgent spiritual steps backward. By creating excessively rigid standards around eating and drinking, we do our personal faith and community of faith a disservice.

Work and play each have an important place for us. Many of us err in the direction of focusing too much on one or the other. We take on more work and responsibility until it crowds out our fun, and at the age of forty, many of us wonder where the spontaneity of earlier years has gone. Others remind themselves too much of a twenty-year-old at the age of forty. A lack of initiative in the storms of life has left them with unrealized dreams and goals. They avoid the inevitable responsibilities of adulthood and remain financially or emotionally dependent on other adults. Still others have found a balance between work and play and adjust their priorities accordingly.

The Teacher in Ecclesiastes lists enjoyment as a separate element of a good life in addition to eating, drinking, and meaningful work. While there is fulfillment in mindful eating and drinking, and joy in meaningful work, there is more to be had when it comes to enjoyment. Those who eat and drink compulsively and impulsively tend to lack a separate category for fun. But we can prioritize enjoyment beyond eating and drinking. Work and financial responsibilities, family relationships, friendships, and community volunteer efforts all add value to our lives. And so does play.

Children are our best teachers when it comes to play because they find their natural curiosity and adventure in the moment without being pulled so readily into the regrets of yesterday or the worries of tomorrow. They rarely are picky about playmates and readily engage with one another despite age, race, and other differences. In at least one instance in scripture, people bring young children to Jesus. When the disciples rebuke the adults and try to send away the children, Jesus asks the disciples to back off and let the children come to him. (See Mark 10:13-15.) He prioritizes their presence and importance. Likewise, Jesus calls us to let the playful, childlike parts of ourselves approach him even when we, like the disciples, may feel that those parts of ourselves are unwelcome. We can approach Jesus as children do, without pretense and without overthinking things. Play brings us into a space that is balanced, unself-conscious, and free.

This reflection speaks directly to those of us who are the responsible caretakers, the go-to people of the world who struggle to make time for play. We spend much of our time addressing others' small- and large-scale problems. Caretakers are adept providers, nurturing friends, and loving parents. We are responsive and loving and seem to have a magnetic pull for people with unbalanced and chaotic lives. Go-to people step up to take care of unpleasant tasks when others will not do them and may have impressive qualifications that intimidate and distance other people. For those of us who prioritize caring for serious responsibilities, play has slowly moved to the bottom of the to-do list, and, as a result, has become almost nonexistent.

When I realized that I was heading in that direction after graduation, I made some attempts to insert play into my life again. I performed in two productions at a community theater in my late twenties, but my greatest lessons in play came a few years later. When I turned thirty, Dusty and I transitioned to a life of babies, sleepless nights, and parenthood. Each of our three sons has taught us an important lesson that has helped us to learn to be better at play. Carlson, our oldest son, thrives with clear expectations and a significant amount of structure. He is brilliant, funny, and has an impeccable memory. Dusty and I live in the moment and often figure out things as we go. We are less the type of people who read the instruction manuals and more the type to dive in and improvise. As we got to know Carlson, we learned to become more structured as we planned ahead for nap times and babysitters. We began to learn the value in routine, and Carlson helped us establish it.

Caleb was born three years later. Constantly laughing and joking, he is a source of creative, joyful companionship. He expresses himself freely and tunes in deeply and expertly to the experiences of other people. He notices the detailed nuance of art and design, and he appreciates the aesthetic. He is full of surprises, and he helps us to pause to laugh and have fun. When Caleb was one, I returned to my Taekwondo training after a twelve-year hiatus. Now he trains with Carlson and me, and we have fun kicking together.

Zach was born when Caleb was two and Carlson was five. Zach spent the entire first two weeks of his life sleeping or cuddling on Dusty's or my chest. We took turns rocking him around the clock. Zach taught us to be still. There was no room for multitasking. He needed stillness, and I had to chuck my perfectionism out the window. In its place came a greater tolerance for a messy house and a greater willingness to be still and embrace the moments I could share with my boys and Dusty. We found that with three young boys, we needed the stillness just as much as Zach did. Zach is now five, and his joyful, infectious, creative ways still remind us to slow down, be still, and enjoy the present moment. He doesn't require the entertainment of toys as he seems to create the fun and be the entertainment wherever he goes. He is fully present in the current moment without worrying about the past or the future.

Though Dusty and I both went from being impressive children to high-achieving students to responsible adults, we learned that there is more to life than productivity. Through our sons, God pointed us toward play and invited us to live more mindfully and have more fun. Play is good for us: The American Academy of Pediatrics has begun to prescribe play. Its research has shown that play's benefits increased problem-solving abilities, empathy, bravery, self-expression, physical strength, and assertiveness.[1]

The Teacher in Ecclesiastes states a clear message about enjoyment, of which play is a part: It is one of the most important parts of life, amid many other aspects of life that are truly "unhappy business." One of the monks I met at the Monastery of the Holy Spirit instructed us to spend time with God in a way that makes the relationship more of a playground experience than a classroom experience. Many of us, he said, approach God as a teacher who will give us a grade. God does not grade us. Instead, God wants to enjoy being with us.

Play requires that we learn the three lessons Dusty and I learned from Carlson, Caleb, and Zach. We can structure our lives to allow room for play. We can rediscover ways to create and prioritize fun. We can make time to be still long enough to know what is fun to us. True play has only one purpose: fun, as an end in itself. Our competitive culture does not readily support play for play's sake alone. But we take a great risk if we allow our lives to omit our play. As psychiatrist Stuart Brown asserts, the opposite of play is not work; it is depression.[2]

One of my playgrounds is the Taekwondo *dojang*. There, I feel playful, free, and challenged. I have a lot of fun. I connect with others, experience variety, and feel an empowering sense of mastery. The stage has also been a playground for me, a place where I could interpret and create and express freely. My favorite chair in our house provides another playground experience when I am playing my ukulele. Playgrounds are the places we can have fun and walk away refreshed, ready to engage again in meaningful work.

What are your playgrounds? Do you need to discover one? Create some time in your life, even if it begins as a ten-minute window, to explore these questions. Consider when and where in your life you have had the most fun and felt the most alive. God will show us the playgrounds where we can thrive. Our maturing faith calls us to find a way to play.

Read Ecclesiastes 9:1-10. Ask yourself three questions: How do I see myself in this story? What is this story teaching me about myself? So what?

Flow

Keep your heart with all vigilance, for from it flow the springs of life.

—Proverbs 4:23

Flow is the psychology of optimal experience. Think of a time in your life when you've been so consumed with what you were doing in a positive and energizing way that you lost a sense of how much time had gone by. What is the thing you'd do just for the sake of doing it? What makes you feel alive? A leading researcher on flow explains that there is no recipe for achieving flow since it is a highly individual experience. However, there are conditions and principles of flow that help encourage someone to experience it. During the state of flow, people tend to feel a sense of order and harmony. There are eight similarities in the experience: The activity that creates the environment for flow is challenging and requires skills, it absorbs you in a positive way, and it is accompanied by clear goals and feedback. The concentration required allows you to lay aside temporarily the concerns of daily life. You have a sense of exercising control in a difficult situation. Time seems to occur on a different dimension, and you lose a sense of self-scrutiny. Doing the activity itself is its own reward. It's freely chosen rather than done to meet external demands.

For example, when I do Taekwondo, I exercise a sense of control over potentially lethal forces. The complex forms I learn challenge me but occur at a pace and in an order that match my skills. I lose a sense of time as I walk into the *dojang*, and there is no room for the frustrations of the day if I am focused and in flow. In sparring, there is constant feedback. I move, or I get kicked. I kick, and I strike or miss my opponent. Taekwondo is not the only activity that helps me to experience flow. Reading with my children, writing, meditating, running, and practicing therapy can also carry me into the optimal state.

We can experience flow, losing a sense of time, by mindfully engaging in the task at hand. The greatest obstacle to flow is letting our attention follow random events, which can lead to feelings of discontent. As we learn to order our consciousness and increase challenges and skills, we create a higher likelihood of experiencing flow. We do so by creating goals and, if needed, breaking down those goals into smaller goals. Doing so creates order out of chaos and allows us to be lost in an activity in a more satisfying way. Within structure, we can relax and experience relief from our default, more chaotic "monkey mind" state of being. We can also move into a flow experience by refining and building our skill set to match the challenges at hand, which helps us avoid boredom. In Taekwondo, I learn increasingly complex forms as I progress in my training. I can continue to refine basic, foundational kicks, strikes, and stances, and I progressively learn more complex kicks and more difficult combinations of movement. Maybe you experience flow playing the guitar by first practicing chords and scales and then learning more complex modes and songs. Maybe you learn to glide on the ice and use fine-tuned strategies to improve your curling technique. There are many activities and methods within each activity that can lead us to a flow experience.

Sometimes chapters of the Christian life become stagnant; they lack flow and look more like disordered attention. This can happen when we are not being challenged by our faith or are not engaging in worship, study, or community that matches our skill set and faith maturity level. When we do not feel like we are progressing in faith, we do not feel absorbed, and we lack goals. We do not seek feedback, and none is given. The challenges and frustrations of daily life flood into our spiritual centers of worship, and we lack a sense of control. We count the number of minutes left in the service and check an obligatory box by attending. It's the opposite of flow.

In contrast, Christ's life was ordered and intentional and reached a complexity that we will likely never be able to fully fathom. In one instance, when Jesus is certainly "hangry" after forty days of fasting in the wilderness, Satan chooses Jesus' intense state of vulnerability to approach him and offer him short-term remedies. Power, sustenance, and wealth can be his if only he'll accept Satan's invitation. Jesus declines all three to embrace God's truths instead. He will not test God; he will not look outside of God for his daily needs; he will not worship Satan. Jesus chooses trust, contentment, and focused worship. (See Luke 4:1-13.)

Jesus then returns to Galilee filled with the power of the Spirit. This seems to be how the process that eventually can lead us to a state of flow works. We persevere, and instead of being spiritually exhausted we are spiritually strengthened. An expert on flow notes that perseverance is probably the most important factor for both success in life and enjoyment of life,[1] which are both major factors in being able to get into a state of flow. Jesus knows perseverance. He becomes fully human and experiences the full range of human emotion, including a need to persevere through temptation.

Flow results in an experience of ourselves that is more complex on two levels: differentiation and integration. Differentiation means that we have become more unique, more autonomous individuals as we've met a challenge that is in line with our goals. But if we only differentiate, we risk becoming self-absorbed. Integration of the self is also necessary to experience a type of complexity that is connected and secure. I believe Jesus lived his life in constant flow. He never lost sight of his purpose and was intensely present with those with whom he talked and interacted.

We waver easily from trust, contentment, and focused worship when left to our own devices. It seems wise to maintain a certain level of distrust out of self-protection. And all around us, we see enticing things that pull us from contentment. People, passions, and career paths invite us to worship them.

To be in flow in our spiritual lives, we need to address the conditions of flow and create a greater sense of complexity where we have grown bored or anxious. Where we are spiritually bored, we can increase our spiritual challenges to experience flow in our relationship with Christ. When we are spiritually anxious, we can work to increase our skill sets: learning more about the Bible, reading commentaries, working toward added discipline and depth in prayer and meditation, or learning to serve and worship in new, more meaningful ways. By facing challenges and building these skill sets, we will experience the flow of our faith.

Read Proverbs 4. Ask yourself three questions: How do I see myself in this story? What is this story teaching me about myself? So what?

Spiritual
Sparring

So Jacob was left alone, and a man wrestled with him till day-break. When the man saw that he could not overpower him, he touched the socket of Jacob's hip so that his hip was wrenched as he wrestled with the man. Then the man said, "Let me go, for it is daybreak." But Jacob replied, "I will not let you go unless you bless me."

—Genesis 32:24-26 (NIV)

I looked into my sparring partner's eyes. She stood across from me, and we bowed to one another out of mutual respect. In full sparring gear, we stood in the ring together. Our Taekwondo Master sounded the command for us to begin, and before I knew what was happening, her foot nailed me square in the head. I recovered physically, but I catapulted backward emotionally. I felt like a child on a playground who had just been knocked down. My tears surfaced, and I fought to choke them back. Physically and emotionally, the kick stung. Her foot left an imprint on my Taekwondo practice. She taught me that I still had a lot to learn about sparring. The bruises and hits I take during a sparring match are both a pain and a blessing. They hurt, but they make me smarter, quicker, and better at Taekwondo.

In meaningful relationships, we spar. We come into conflict and must be willing to acknowledge and engage in it in a way that is neither avoidant nor harmful. We can carefully assess our partner by staying attuned to how the other's words and actions impact us and by expressing what we want and need with honesty and integrity. We take up space and assert ourselves with a kihap, but we have to be willing to spar too. In Taekwondo we spar with our teammates and wear appropriate protective gear. We are not seeking to hurt one another, but we do compete and kick hard. In relationships, we need to wear appropriate gear too. We need boundaries and limits, and we make self-protective choices.

I used to share my heart readily even before a friendship reached a level of trust that could tolerate it. Because I desired close relationships, I would confide in people, see the best in people, and hope for the best. Sometimes that strategy backfired. We benefit when we get to know someone and build trust before sharing our more intimate and vulnerable selves. We are wise to recognize patterns of behavior that alert and remind us of those who have hurt and betrayed us in the past so that we do not repeat problematic relationship patterns. When we walk into relationships with blinders on, we may receive a painful kick to the head. We need our "gear" of emotional self-care and boundaries.

We benefit from being flexible and adaptable by doing what works. In Taekwondo, adaptability means changing your stance in the sparring ring when you get kicked so that you don't keep getting kicked. We can practice changing our stance in relationships through an alternating rhythm between relaxation and intensity. We need a regular plan and schedule for calming relaxation since we cannot thrive in constant intensity. On the other hand, we need some challenges and intensity and the courage to step out and try new things.

Sparring can be intense and playful all at once. God seems to want to interact with us in the same way. The Bible recounts a sparring story between Jacob and God. Jacob recounts that he sees "God face to face" (Gen. 32:30). Jacob's brother, Esau, is coming to meet with him after Jacob has tricked their father into giving the blessing to him instead of Esau. Jacob has stolen Esau's rightful blessing as the elder son. Jacob fears Esau's anger. He sends gifts to Esau ahead of him to try to appease Esau's anger before they meet. That same night, Jacob sends his wives, maids, children, and all his belongings across a stream and is left alone. I wonder what prompts him to want to be alone. Maybe he senses danger or knows that there is a struggle that requires some separation from everything familiar to him to work out. While he is alone, a man wrestles with Jacob and knocks Jacob's hip out of its socket. Jacob does not back down; he insists on receiving a blessing from God. Because of Jacob's persistence, God grants him a blessing and a new name. Regardless of the deception and betrayal he brings to his family, Jacob is not beyond God's blessing. It takes all night and he acquires an injury, but Jacob walks away with the blessing he seeks.

We do not know the nature of the unnamed conflict. We do not know whether the wrestling begins as a playful sparring match, as one between two brothers, or whether God's anger is roused. We do not know why the broken hip is necessary. All we know is that all in one night, after encountering God, Jacob walks away with a limp and a blessing. Often, so do we.

I used to fear confrontation and avoid it. When I anticipated anger or disapproval, I would often withdraw and spend time alone, as Jacob did. In those moments, I hoped that God would comfort me; but sometimes I encountered the same frustration with God that I had with people. I wanted a blessing but instead received a spiritual injury in the form of God's silence and apparent unavailability. I felt a lack of peace and a lack of love. I assumed that God was capable of comforting me but was withholding that comfort. I could not make sense of it. I withdrew even more or coped in ways that I knew were not real solutions, unmindfully eating or drinking or distracting myself. But eventually, I engaged with God anyway in some small way. I picked up the Bible and read a proverb, uttered a reluctant prayer, attended a church service, or talked to a spiritually insightful friend who would tell me the things I needed to hear. I found that spiritual persistence eventually brings spiritual peace. God was not waiting for me with a warm hug and a "Bless her heart." God loves me enough to spar. Through my reengagement with God, I saw that I needed to do the difficult things. In love, God prompted me to lift my head up and get myself back on the sparring mat rather than avoid discomfort. I needed to confront people sometimes, feel complex emotions, and acknowledge uncomfortable truths about the dynamics that I contributed in my conflicts with others. The experience of discomfort is the wound, but the outcome holds a blessing. By acknowledging uncomfortable truths and feelings, I could let go, resolve conflicts, and move forward with more self-awareness. In the end, a spiritual sparring match involves both a wound and a blessing.

God acts in unexpected ways or seems absent when we most want and need God's presence. We spar with God when we doubt, when we lament, and when we question God's will and intention for our lives. We may feel God's timing is off, or wonder why circumstances such as loss, crisis, and injury arise. We may feel anger, sadness, and disappointment. These feelings and experiences may be the wounds of our sparring match with God, but we can persist through the encounter and may emerge with the sought-after blessing. When we are willing to face God with persistence, wrestle with God, and enter into the intensity of a spiritual sparring match, we can expect wounds as well as blessings. As an unexpected kick to the head made me a smarter and more strategic fighter, a wound from God may itself be the blessing.

Read Genesis 32. Ask yourself three questions: How do I see myself in this story? What is this story teaching me about myself? So what?

Just Visiting

Jesus said to her, "Everyone who drinks of this water will be thirsty again, but those who drink of the water that I will give them will never be thirsty."'

—John 4:13-14

On a hot day, Jesus sits on the ground by a well. A Samaritan woman comes to draw water, and Jesus asks her for a drink. The woman is astonished. The cultural climate deems Jesus' actions highly inappropriate. It is unacceptable for him to be talking with a woman, and even less acceptable for him, a Jew, to be talking to a Samaritan woman. Nevertheless, he steps across cultural barriers and asks her for a drink. As they continue talking about the well water, Jesus takes the opportunity to speak to her about living water. Jesus says to her, "Everyone who drinks of this water will be thirsty again, but those who drink of the water that I will give them will never be thirsty. The water that I will give will become in them a spring of water gushing up to eternal life" (John 4:13-14). She replies, "Sir, give me this water, so that I may never be thirsty or have to keep coming here to draw water" (John 4:15). Jesus knows the woman has had multiple failed marriages, five to be exact. Things are not working out well for her relationally, and it may look a little shady for Jesus to be engaging her in conversation. But Jesus extends living water to address her thirst. He identifies himself as the Messiah and speaks of the spiritual nature of living water versus the temporary fulfillment of well water. Her short-lived relationships are the well water, and they only satisfy temporarily. But we can all know the living water that keeps us at a calm baseline. From there, we can visit excitement, but come back to a place we want to be.

At a mental health conference, a man I'll call Will shared his story of addiction and recovery. Will had more than twenty years of sobriety from marijuana, cocaine, and heroin. He spoke about a powerful personal experience of finding his breath in yoga. He found recovery from years of quenching thirst through an altered state. Will spoke about *visiting* excitement in sobriety. He *visited,* then returned to a baseline, calm experience. I understood his thirst for an altered state. At times I preferred an altered state above the company of my feelings too. There were times when my baseline, unaltered experience didn't appeal to me at all. It felt chaotic, tense, and self-critical. Altered states called to me to come and drink, and I did. Altered states, as anyone who's encountered them knows, promise but fail to deliver the living water to which the Bible points us.

Our challenge is to find a baseline experience of contentment in Jesus where there is lasting refreshment. Coming to Jesus over and over, in each moment, is the first important step. Jesus provides living water in great supply, if only we will come and drink. Coming to Jesus means praying and acknowledging thirst. Believing means knowing Jesus can satisfy the thirst. Drinking means being willing to receive an uncomfortable amount of compassion and love. Our culture bends over backward convincing us that living water exists in things we buy, attain, consume, and accomplish. As we seek play and pursue flow, and as we engage in spiritual sparring matches, we need to return again and again to our baseline experience of drinking from the eternal source of life. We can visit the excitement of play and the flow of faith but always need to return to a place where Jesus quenches thirst. There, we can finally be calm, in a baseline contentment of embracing ourselves in ways that allow us to embrace others more fully and authentically.

For some of us, our childhood homes were chaotic and intense. A calm baseline experience did not exist. Those who grew up in this situation can find it particularly challenging to identify what a calm baseline looks like as an adult. An emotional baseline is balanced. It does not involve an absence of intense emotion; rather, a healthy emotional baseline includes a full range of human emotion accompanied by permission to feel it and positive strategies for coping with it. For instance, when I hear sad news or have a sad experience, I may cry and feel down for a period of time. But my sadness does not launch me into a self-destructive episode or keep me from performing my responsibilities at work and home. Sadness does not veer me off course or immobilize me. I can also feel fear, joy, and anger as part of my baseline experience. They are the emotions of daily life, and while they can be intense, they need not derail me. When sadness immobilizes us and throws us off course, when anger leads to poor decisions, or when fear leads to excessive avoidance, we can and should reach out for help and emotional support.

A spiritually calm baseline faith involves self-discipline and self-control, with or without emotional highs. Like a healthy emotional baseline, a healthy spiritual baseline includes a range of experiences from spiritually dry to spiritually fulfilling. It includes doubt and uncertainty, questions, and hope. It includes the days and moments we feel less than passionate about God and faith but show up anyway. We crack open our Bibles and read something that doesn't particularly stir our souls. We sit in a church service and may just feel distracted by the people around us or by our own thoughts. We hear a thoughtful spiritual insight and may or may not put it into practice. While the high, Spirit-filled emotions of faith are absent, so is the chaos of life apart from God. We have a routine and we follow it, but we remain flexible and open to hearing or pursuing something we didn't expect. Sometimes we feel a prompting from God or from scripture, or a person speaks to us and we feel and learn something powerful. We visit excitement through playing, flowing, or sparring. But in the many moments when we do the less exciting structuring of our schedules to allow time for play, strive for but don't reach a state of flow, or notice an absence of meaningful sparring, our faith still remains in a baseline spiritual state. The baseline of faith ebbs and moves forward, even when we are not playing, flowing, or sparring.

Read John 4:1-42. Ask yourself three questions: How do I see myself in this story? What is this story teaching me about myself? So what?

Remain in Me

Remain in me, as I also remain in you. No branch can bear fruit by itself; it must remain in the vine. Neither can you bear fruit unless you remain in me.

—John 15:4 (NIV)

Early in our marriage, Dusty and I served as premarital mentors for other couples. Admittedly, our experiences were limited at that point, but we did our best to share what we learned about life on the other side of the tied knot. Three months after we began dating, Dusty got down on one knee and offered me a diamond ring on an ivy-covered bridge in downtown Indianapolis. Nine short months later we walked down the aisle, simply because we felt sure. We spent our first year in a humble residence we nicknamed The Blueplex, trying to make marriage work while Dusty completed his undergraduate degree. I started my graduate program at Ball State, and we mostly lived on my student stipend while we navigated married life and tried to help others do the same.

Psychologist John Gottman asserts that couples suffer when criticism, contempt, defensiveness, and emotional shutdowns become commonplace.[1] When any of these negative patterns emerge, a couple's desire can fade. The spouse becomes someone to take care of or please, and a parent-child dynamic replaces the lover's dynamic. The couple fails to feel the sense of deep connection that they once shared. Psychologist Esther Perel proposes that playing a caretaking role kills desire, which is why it is vital for married couples to function as two healthy, independent adults. Caretaking is an appropriate role for an adult to provide for a child or elder, but if one spouse plays a parental role with the other, intimacy tends to suffer.[2] Couples become one flesh (see Genesis 2:24) but remain two separate people with two separate personalities and two different collections of passions, goals, and preferences. Separateness and differences can be celebrated. They allow desire to thrive.

Couples often expect passion to unfold spontaneously as it did earlier in the relationship. Couples therapists often recommend scheduling date nights to boost a couple's feelings of intimacy. Regularly scheduled efforts to increase closeness set the foundation for passionate encounters. The same strategy applies when it comes to building greater closeness with God. We get caught up in spiritually romantic ideals of being powerfully moved by the Holy Spirit in prayer. That can happen, but usually it doesn't.

Schedule a time to connect to Jesus. Consider when your best energy and focus occur. I focus best in the morning, while Dusty focuses best at night. Nearly eleven years into our lives as parents, we realized that it made sense for me to take the lead getting the kids up and ready for school in the morning and for him to take the lead getting each of them settled into bed at night. The things that are most important to us should be done at the times when we have the most and best energy. Every day we have an opportunity to use our best time for the things we value most. We can wait to do the leftover tasks, like laundry and dishes, with leftover energy.

Recognize when your best energy occurs, and set aside focused time, even if it is ten minutes, to spend with God. Personal self-disclosure through prayer is a good place to start. The other part of the interaction is taking time to listen to God's thoughts and feelings about what we disclose. We can listen for God's voice through silent reflection, Bible study, meditating on God's Word, and talking with spiritually wise and centered people. The more you get to know God, the better you will recognize God's voice. Make time to listen today, and grow in intimacy with God.

One of the ways we can grow in intimacy with God is by following God's commandment, which Jesus lays out in John 15 as "love one another." Jesus tells us that we can remain in him and experience joy when we love one another as he has loved us. Loving others happens best when it comes from the energy supplied by being connected to Jesus, the vine. He is the vine, and we are the branches. When we connect with God through prayer, Bible study, and community with other believers, the ability to love flows through the empowerment we receive from the vine.

When I walk through the door after a long day of work, I often see a scattering of Legos, snacks, unfolded laundry, homework, costumes, dishes, and books. Love means taking two or three deep breaths and hugging Dusty and the boys, asking how their days were, looking them in the eyes and connecting with them, and trying to really understand how they are doing. Love means telling them the truth about how I am doing. Putting people before tasks, being kind instead of being right, and removing the log in my own eye before examining the speck in theirs are a few ways I love my family. Loving others means looking for the truth and not keeping score. Love may mean cancelling or rescheduling my preferred plans to make allowance for others' needs. It may mean saying yes or saying no. When we are connected to Jesus, the vine, we experience his love and can let that love flow into the lives of those around us.

Read John 15:1-17. Ask yourself three questions: How do I see myself in this story? What is this story teaching me about myself? So what?

WEEKEND PRACTICE

Experience Play and Flow

Consider whether your relationship with God has felt more like a playground experience or a classroom experience. This weekend, identify and implement more modes of play in your life and take steps to move yourself toward a flow experience. Think of flow as a way of identifying with and connecting to Christ as your vine of sustenance and life.

First, identify an experience from your past that brought great joy, so much so that you lost track of time and felt completely immersed in the experience. Name the experience that comes to mind first, even if it occurred long ago. It can be an experience from childhood, adolescence, or adulthood. Consider whether some version of that experience could be part of your life again now.

Second, carve out time in your schedule for play. An example would be "every Tuesday evening from 8:00-10:00 p.m." Write it in your calendar as though it were an event for which you had to show up. Even if you don't yet know how that time will look, schedule a time for play in order to prioritize it. If you have a significant other, try to arrange a time each week that each of you can devote to play. If you have children, consider hiring a babysitter or trading off with another couple or friend weekly or monthly. Playing together as a couple may involve running an obstacle course race together, a date night of music, or a pottery lesson. Try to think of a fun activity beyond going to dinner or out for a drink or shopping. Independent play may involve taking an introductory lesson in a new sport, strolling through an independent bookstore, going for a swim, or playing an instrument. Playing looks different for each couple and each person. What sounds fun to me may not sound fun at all to you, and fun is the essential component of play. Actively participate in something like a game or a sport rather than passively observing. If you can set aside your evaluative and productivity-minded inner voice and instead embrace curiosity and adventure, you will be on the right track, no matter what activity you choose.

When your scheduled time comes, reflect on your memory of play. Do the closest thing you can think of that resembles that memory. Try to approach the scheduled time as a time of exploration rather than seeking to accomplish anything in particular. Realize that it may take some trial and error to discover what is fun for you. At the end of your scheduled time, reflect and learn. How much fun did you have? Is the activity something you'd like to do again? Use what you know for your next scheduled time.

After at least your first few times set aside for play and flow, do some journaling. Here are some suggested questions to guide you:

1. Are you comfortable playing, just for the sake of playing?
2. How readily do you grant yourself permission to play?
3. Why is play important in your faith journey?

WEEK SIX: WHAT IS NEXT FOR YOU

A Carpenter's
Work

I am confident of this, that the one who began a good work among
you will bring it to completion by the day of Jesus Christ.
—Philippians 1:6

I grew up in the small town of Mahomet, Illinois, surrounded by farmland.
When I was eight, we moved into the Woodfield West house, where I spent
the remainder of my childhood and adolescence. From my bedroom window
I watched the trees we planted in that yard grow until they towered over our
heads. A tornado whipped through and uprooted a tree from the front yard leaving only a hole with undisturbed weeds around it. I crashed my bike and ended
up with stitches in my knee. I celebrated the day I got my driver's license, and I
took countless free throw shots in the driveway. It was the place I called home for
ten years. I lived and slept there, grew up there, and dreamed there.

One Sunday night in my mid-thirties, I had a dream that I believe gave me a
glimpse of Jesus. I dreamed that I had gone back to my hometown to visit a friend
and to work on restoring my old house with plans to eventually move there. In
the dream, the house was my Woodfield West house, but it looked different than
it did when I lived there during my school years. When I pulled into the driveway, I parked my car and approached the house. It was nestled behind several big
trees. I entered the house and looked around. It obviously was being renovated.

I expected that I would be alone, but I entered a room and saw a man hammering and working on renovations to the space. He had the kind of presence that puts you immediately at ease, so I didn't feel worried or unsafe. He seemed to know me and seemed sincerely glad to see me. He remarked that he was sorry he'd missed my earlier visits. I knew he was there to work on the house too. I asked him about the history of the house, and he said that he had once lived there and showed me to his favorite room, the room that had been his bedroom. Though it was bare and in need of further renovation, it had a natural and simplistic coziness. The ceiling angled upward on both sides and came to a point in the middle. There were wooden beams and a loft between the A-frame. His work was slow, steady, and purposeful. He was not hurried or frustrated. Though there was much work to do, he didn't seem overwhelmed or discouraged. Instead, he worked with a loving intentionality.

He sought and encouraged my active involvement in the work. As we worked together, we talked effortlessly. He had a joyful and deeply authentic presence. I felt the type of comfort you'd feel with someone you've known all your life. As we worked on cleaning off one of the beams, I was aware of my insecurities and struggles. Suddenly, I felt self-conscious. Flustered, I dropped a pile of screws, and they scattered onto the floor. There was not a hint of judgment on his part as he bent down to help me pick up everything I'd dropped. I felt supported, affirmed, and empowered to continue in the work.

Upon awakening from this very vivid dream, I began telling Dusty the details. I stopped in mid-sentence, struck by its spiritual significance. Scriptures surfaced in my mind about Jesus preparing "a place for me" and his occupation as a carpenter. (See John 14:3; Mark 6:3.) I thought of the reality of being a work in progress. I know that God will continue working on me and refining my weak areas. God does the work slowly, steadily, and lovingly.

In my professional therapy practice, I integrate solution-focused therapy into my work with clients.[1] One foundational belief within the theory is that we construct the solutions and outcomes in our lives. If we are the builders of our lives, our lives could be seen as homes we inhabit during the years we are here on earth. As builders, we can choose to be purposeful in the materials we use or we can cut corners. We can attend to problems as they surface or ignore them until they turn into bigger problems. As I work with clients, I can see them building a future, an emotionally healthier existence for themselves. I have done the same work. It takes a foundation of commitment to sit with discomfort and a willingness to use some trial and error to find the unique blend of coping skills that work as a new framework for thinking about ourselves and the world. The therapy process parallels a building project in countless ways, including the tendency for it to take much longer than expected.

I am aware of the benefit of approaching myself in the same patient and nonjudgmental way as the man in my dream approached me. God approaches us in this way with patience and love. As we participate in God's work each day, loving ourselves despite our insecurities, and as we patiently come alongside ourselves to pick up the pieces when we drop them into a scattered mess, we stay fully invested in the present moment and do the work of God.

For many years I faced the challenges of perfectionism: I held myself up to impossibly high standards and was prone to self-criticism. Perfection is unachievable, and the quest for perfection is isolating. The more set on the quest for perfection I become, the more fearful I am of exposing my vulnerabilities. To be alone in any struggle magnifies its power and prolongs the time it takes to heal. I strive to remain mindful of the times in life when I have taken the risk to reveal my vulnerability to someone I trust. When a friend embraces me and we share our imperfect but nonetheless beautiful lives, I walk away lighter and more energized. Healing happens.

I stay mindful of that image of the man in my dream who collaborated with me on the renovations of my childhood home. Though I expected to be alone in the project, he was with me teaching me to be gentle and kind with myself in the work I was doing. As a problem-solver and one who is prone to analyzing and overthinking most things, I am calmed as I think about his patient and thoughtful work. Not rushed. Not harried. Not checking his phone for his next appointment. He was just present, actively participating and enjoying the process.

Jesus comes alongside us with compassion in our internal renovations as well. As we navigate uncertainty, make messes, and try to build something new on the emotional foundation we've been given, we can find companionship and love in the process. We can come alongside ourselves with compassion and understand that Jesus approaches us with compassion too. Jesus calmly and lovingly crouches down to help us pick up our messes, with a silent understanding that says, "Me too."

Read John 14:1-17. Ask yourself three questions: How do I see myself in this story? What is this story teaching me about myself? So what?

Creating Faith

*A stream would rise from the earth, and water the whole face of the ground—then the L*ORD *God formed man from the dust of the ground, and breathed into his nostrils the breath of life; and the man became a living being.*

—Genesis 2:6-7

Now in my forties, I'm in the transition between early and middle adulthood. I was a student during much of young adulthood, and I now see myself falling naturally into roles as a supervisor, professor, and mother of elementary-school-aged children. At this stage of life, I seem to have endless opportunities for giving that need to be balanced out with some less productive and more reflective periods of time to avoid overextension. Our churches provide ample opportunity for volunteering, and each of us faces the challenge of how much to give. I have found it helpful to ask myself these questions: *What is God calling me, with my specific gifts, to do? What do I feel most passionate about pursuing in my life of faith?* My question for myself cannot be *Is this a good thing to do?* because there are endless good opportunities for giving, and with too many *yes*es we can burn out quickly. We also cannot just ask ourselves the question *What do I want to do?* as we may limit ourselves by our comfort zones and personal preferences.

The Bible tells us that we begin as dust and God breathes life into us. (See Genesis 2:7.) Because we are created in God's image, we are created with purpose and we help create. The two Creation accounts in Genesis reveal God's creative power, God's ability to make order out of chaos, and God's valuing of beauty, design, and relationship. These aspects of God's creative power and of our part in it shine brightly throughout the narrative of the Genesis story.

The book of Genesis was compiled from several literary sources, and the resulting book has a beauty and complexity not unlike the natural world it describes. Genesis has been considered "a layered mosaic of meanings"[1] that transcends any one story or source. The two Creation accounts in the Bible do not line up entirely, so some say they are in contradiction. In the first account of Creation, known as the priestly account, God creates light, water, land, fruit and vegetation, sun and moon, and people during the first six days. Finally, God rests on the seventh day. (See Genesis 1:1–2:4.) A great deal of energy has been spent on answering questions about the exact time line of Creation. Was it seven days, seven eras, or on some other time line altogether? I believe the account of God's creation of the world in Genesis has less to do with a minute-by-minute calendar, and more to do with showing us the nature of God. The second account of Creation tells of a stream rising and covering the earth. Then God creates a man, then the garden, then animals, and then a woman. (See Genesis 2:5–25.) The order and method are different. We can get caught up in the specifics, or we can embrace the similarities. In both accounts, God brings life to a place where life is not present, creates people in God's image, and creates order.

God brings life and order to our individual lives as well. We can read the priestly, seven-day Creation story as an illustration of the way our individual spiritual lives unfold. On the first day, God separates light from darkness. Likewise, our lives are separated by two spiritual realities: We are created in God's image, and we are born into a world where there is sin, in which we will take part. These two capacities coexist. We are created in both spiritual light and spiritual darkness.

On the second day, God separates the waters above from the waters below. As every person who has given or witnessed birth knows, breaking water is how life lurches forth from the womb. Just as we need the right balance of amniotic fluid surrounding us within a mother's uterus, we continue to need water throughout the rest of our lives. As my son Carlson pointed out while learning about the water cycle in his fourth-grade science class, water never goes away. Though water cycles through various forms, it remains. God knows we need a constant source of life that may take many forms. One of our first tasks of life is building a sense of trust that our caregivers will provide consistent, loving support in various material and spiritual forms.

On the third day, God creates dry land and clusters the waters together into seas. God summons the earth to put forth trees, plants, and fruit with seeds.

God's creation has a cyclic, self-sustaining nature. Seeds bring forth more fruit. Land gives us a place to call home. We value our real estate, and we seek desirable places to settle and thrive. We labor and produce more fruit. We plant and water. As we do so, we witness and experience spiritual, physical, and emotional growth.

On the fourth day, God creates the sun, moon, and stars for light and to give signs, order, and seasons. In our spiritual lives, we identify our sources of light. We see the love of God shining through relationships and spiritual experiences. At the same time, we cycle through periods of darkness in our faith when we feel down and discouraged and when we struggle to hear God's voice. We cycle through spiritual light and darkness as the seasons of our lives unfold.

On the fifth day, God summons fish to the waters and birds to the sky. God knows we will visit both highs and lows in our faith journey. Some days we soar with success and good fortune; other days we visit the depths of the silent sea. Both have a place in the creation of our faith journeys.

On the sixth day, God creates wild animals, cattle, and all types of creeping creatures. Then, God creates people to be companions of one another and entrusts them with all of God's creation. In our spiritual lives, we accept responsibility for what God entrusts to us. We discover relationships. We make choices about how to care for the people, places, and roles that God gives us.

God makes order out of chaos with great variety and complexity. God stands back, assesses the created work, and calls it "good" (Gen. 1:31). Then God rests. God sets the first precedent for engaging in an alternating rhythm of creative work followed by restful reflection. Both are necessary parts of life. We need an outlet for challenging, creative work, and we need time to step back and assess whether it is "good."

Whether we reflect on our work at the end of a long life or are forced to consider our place in the world as we realize our life may be cut short by illness or injury, we spend time assessing our creative work: Has it been good? Have we brought order where there was chaos, light where there was darkness, life where none existed? In the end, will we rest and call it "good"?

No matter our current life stage, we can all consider what we have created or will create with our life. We can make time to reflect on the stage of creation that speaks to us. As we identify our place in creation, we can make space for our creative passions to flow into our life of faith. Then we can allow our God-given creativity to flow from our heart into the lives of others. We can create a life lived in God's image.

Read Genesis 1–2. Ask yourself three questions: How do I see myself in this story? What is this story teaching me about myself? So what?

Withstanding the Floodwaters

The flood continued forty days on the earth; and the waters increased, and bore up the ark, and it rose high above the earth. The waters swelled and increased greatly on the earth; and the ark floated on the face of the waters.

—Genesis 7:17-18

N oah's story teaches us that before the floods rise, we need to build something that will withstand them. We need God's guidance to build something that will last. In therapy, we use emotional "tools" to manage distress, gain relationship skills, regulate emotion, and remain mindful.[1] When the floods come, our emotional arks built with these tools can help us withstand the floods of personal, family, and cultural struggles. Time spent journaling, attending and engaging in therapy, or in prayer and meditation may seem a waste of time to some, but they are the spiritual and emotional tools that help us withstand the trials that will surely flood our lives at some point, if they have not already.

God gives Noah the ultimate challenge to build the ark, and God gives Noah the information and instruction he needs to build it, down to the cubit. (See Genesis 6:15.) God will instruct us in what we need to know to keep ourselves afloat. It is up to us, as it was up to Noah, to worry less about others' perceptions and more about preparing ourselves to receive and act on God's information. We can pick up the spiritual tools God offers and construct a life built on a strong self-identity in God's faithfulness that will protect us when the storms of life begin to surge.

I imagine that many of the people around Noah think he is crazy to build a huge boat and talk about an impending flood without rain. We do the same to the people around us today. Many of us have a friend, colleague, or family member who has a big dream, one that they fully embrace and pour all their resources into while others stand by with skeptical glances and question the methods or general judgment of the venture. As onlookers, we wait to see if things will play out in the way we predicted, but we don't lose much sleep over it and mostly move on with our own lives. We know others who talk constantly of the next "flood"—a political candidate or party who has taken control or seems about to take control, nuclear threats, the details of a new tax plan, or an opioid crisis. In 1999, many of us went to great lengths to prepare for the new millennium, and some of us convinced ourselves that catastrophic events would occur on January 1, 2000. Throughout the world, many people fear the next actual flood as predicted by the path of the next hurricane. Others fear a more personal, internal flood, unleashed by a newly disclosed family secret.

We each choose which floods to acknowledge and take seriously. We each choose a way to respond to the next flood that surges through our culture. We decide first whether it is a true threat or merely something that will occur with little direct consequence to us. We may choose to pretend it's not happening, to get lost in our own self-absorbed routines of life and refuse to be interrupted. We may instead invest in preventing the flood and warning everyone else that it is coming. If we pay attention, beyond the echoes of self-curated journalism and opinions of neighbors, we may hear a nudge from God, who is ready to fully equip us for the next flood.

When faced with a flood, we can get distracted from the spiritual practices that sustain us. Though Noah faces a world-ending flood, he does not seem to become anxious. He does not allow himself any distractions from the secure promise of God's provision. When we feel overpowered by the surges of the floods around us, we can follow Noah's example and trust in the security of what God asks us to build in our lives.

In the book of Acts, Gamaliel, a respected teacher of the law, observes the work and lives of the apostles. He warns the people, "Keep away from these men and let them alone; because if this plan or this undertaking is of human origin, it will fail; but if it is of God, you will not be able to overthrow them—in that case you may even be found fighting against God!" (Acts 5:38-39). If God is behind the work in our lives, it will not fail. When we resist God's work in our lives, we

may as well be fighting God directly. Noah builds a ridiculously huge boat on
dry land, but God knows the flood is coming, and Noah listens.

When we see a flood on the horizon, we may look for an easy, short-term fix
that does well enough for now while ignoring the truth of the impending storm.
Instead, we can ask God what to build for ourselves and our family, and how to
build it. We can be proactive and invest in long-term security based on what we
hear from God about how to use our life and our resources. When we listen for
God's direction that may make little sense to us or to observers in the short-term,
we will be safe and able to care for God's creation when the waters rise. Consider
what you need to build today, gather your tools, and begin the project.

Read Genesis 6:5–7:24. Ask yourself three questions: How do I see myself
in this story? What is this story teaching me about myself? So what?

Knock, Knock

Ask, and it will be given you; search, and you will find; knock, and the door will be opened for you. For everyone who asks receives, and everyone who searches finds, and for everyone who knocks, the door will be opened.

—Matthew 7:7-8

During my sophomore year of college, I found myself in a lonely situation where most of my close friends were in relationships but I was not dating anyone. As a result, they had default plans that involved time alone with their significant other for almost any weekend night while I wrestled with the question of why I wanted but did not have a boyfriend. I felt ready to invest in a healthy relationship, and I felt lonely.

One Friday night I had an empty calendar and wanted to be with a friend. I went to a few friends' doors in the dorm early in the evening to see if I could find someone who was available. I knocked but heard silence. The corridor had a ghost-town feel of emptiness and plans that were taking place elsewhere. Closed door after closed door represented people with fun lives. My own life seemed to stand in stark contrast, and my inner critical voice reached a crescendo that convinced me that no one cared about me or about my lonely Friday. Finally, my friend across the hall answered her door. We talked, listened to music, and had a great evening as we laughed about the realities of life. Sharing laughter and understanding one another's life challenges was enough of a solution for the evening.

When I remember this evening so many years ago, my persistence strikes me. I had to continue to knock to experience the evening I had wanted. I do not always show that kind of persistence, but in that instance I did. And it paid off.

Many times in my own therapy process I have felt like my work is getting repetitive: I have been here and thought this before. I revisit struggles that I thought I had overcome already, that I feel I *should* have overcome. So many clients I see express the same frustration. They feel they have not come far enough beyond their personal thorns; it's a familiar feeling.

Change occurs on the path of a slinky-like spiral rather than on a stepwise, linear path.[1] We take steps forward but then experience a setback. We revisit our familiar vulnerabilities over and over again. But as with the slinky, each revolution is from a slightly different place. The spiral is heading upward, slowly but surely; when the slinky uses all its rotations, it can work as a whole and travel down a flight of stairs. Each revolution, each path of revisiting our challenges from a slightly different place, gives us added perspective, tools, and life experiences so we are never back at square one. When we find ourselves in a familiar emotional struggle, we can remember that it's to be expected and look for the slight change in perspective and opportunity to learn that was not apparent or available during our last cycle through the struggle. Each rotation is a knock on the door of change. Eventually, a door will open.

Too often, we approach spirituality in a passive way, as if we can wait around watching others' lives unfold until the day when the mail carrier will hand us our life's purpose, addressed from God. The psalmist tells us to "count our days" (Ps. 90:12). We are to be mindful that while we don't know how many days we have, the number is limited. It's up to us to take action and make each day count. We do not have time to be weighed down by self-criticism. In Philippians, Paul calls us to "work out [our] own salvation with fear and trembling" (2:12). God knows it will be an arduous process but invites us to take an active role in working it out. When we keep knocking, we will eventually get an answer.

Read Matthew 7:1-14. Ask yourself three questions: How do I see myself in this story? What is this story teaching me about myself? So what?

Acting in the Unknown

"What no eye has seen, nor ear heard, nor the human heart conceived, what God has prepared for those who love him"—these things God has revealed to us through the Spirit.

—1 Corinthians 2:9-10

When I lead therapy groups, we start with a brief check-in, where every group member gives a brief introduction and says how connected they feel to themselves, physically and emotionally. They assign a number from one to ten that describes how connected they feel in that particular moment. Along with their one-to-ten rating, every group member shares a word or phrase that describes their most present fear or obstacle. One of the most commonly identified fears has to do with uncertainty. Clients regularly ask themselves, *When will I get better? Is it possible?* While the nature of our fears differs, we all deal with fear of the future at times. We ask whether our children will be safe and make good choices as they take steps of independence, whether our next career decision will turn out to be a good one, whether we will get married, have a child, have another child, graduate, enjoy true love, achieve success, or maintain health and live a long life.

I encourage my clients not to retreat from uncertainty but to embrace it. Uncertainty opens up room for risk, adventure, and joy to unfold. Uncertainty means acknowledging our human limitations, while resting in the peace that transcends understanding (see Philippians 4:7), the peace of knowing God has all our concerns in mind and that "in everything God works for good with those who love him, who are called according to his purpose" (Rom. 8:28, RSV). We may find relief when we stop ruminating about the past, stop rehearsing for the future, and rest in the present moment of uncertainty. We hold on to what we can in the moment, but even the moment needs to be released into the hands of God.

Faith in God requires a willingness to act on what we know despite what we do not know. The book of Acts, which was probably written by Luke, recounts a story about Philip that illustrates readiness to act after a prompting from God. Philip is an evangelist who preaches, performs miracles, and has a special role in caring for the poor. One of Philip's shining moments occurs when he responds to an internal prompt from the Holy Spirit to approach a stranger in a carriage, an Ethiopian eunuch. The eunuch appears to have difficulty interpreting scripture as he reads it aloud. Philip acts with a moment's notice. He breaks out of his plan and agenda for the day to respond to a silent but sure prompting from God urging him to approach the carriage, sit beside the eunuch, and help him interpret the scripture. The Spirit leads Philip to a brief but meaningful encounter that transforms the eunuch's life as he begins to fully contemplate the scripture and asks on the spot to be baptized. (See Acts 8:26-40.)

When we face unknowns, we can go back to focusing on what we *do* know. When I felt ambivalent about an upcoming career decision, one of my closest friends and I got together for dinner and talked about it. Over a glass of wine, I mulled over my uncertainty about which decision represented God's will for me. My friend, a fellow psychologist, often opens the window of clarity and wisdom to help me consider an additional, valuable perspective. She pointed to the information I already know for sure about myself, my interests, and my passions. She suggested I stop waiting to discern a calling. She said, "Why don't *you* call *it*?" She knows me well, and her words stirred my reluctance. Something clicked. It became clear that my passivity wasn't an act of faith but a failure to trust what I already knew. God had given me enough information; I needed to actively engage with God, not wait for a sign.

During graduate school, I studied research on the use of faith and religion as coping strategies. I quickly discovered that people use faith and religion in various ways to cope with various stressful life events like health problems and major transitions. The literature on religious coping shows that some strategies are negative and some are positive when it comes to achieving better psychological health. The strategies that work best include using faith and religion to find purpose in suffering. Giving and receiving support in a religious community also works. People who seek a sense of control through a partnership with God or who do what they can and give the rest to God fare much better than those who simply wait for God to act or who plead with God for a miracle.[1]

Perhaps we should ask for a miracle we can help create ourselves through a partnership with God. Maybe *we* choose the miracle as it unfolds within God's purposes. I see miracles happen in small ways every day: My child finally understands why it's important to brush his teeth. A client tries a feared food and finds, to her surprise, that she does not gain excessive weight and can tolerate the feeling of fullness. A friend finally says no to taking on too many commitments and allows herself to take some well-deserved time off. My child looks at me and says he always comes to me for help with problems because I am so good at helping him work out his feelings.

If a miracle occurs tonight while you are sleeping, and you wake up tomorrow and have everything you have ever wanted, how would you know that the miracle had happened? What would you be doing differently? Steve de Shazer asks his clients a version of this question and has found that his clients are able to describe in great detail what they want in their lives. Clients spend entire sessions describing their miracles. Each miracle is different.[2] Then, de Shazer asks each client which parts of the miracle are already occurring. No matter how much we may struggle, we probably are doing something successfully, creating some small piece of our own miracle. It may not feel significant to us in this moment, but we can note what it is and keep doing it. Small changes lead to bigger changes. Through the small pieces of our miracles that are already happening, we interact with God's loving intentions for us, and the process continues to unfold.

Read Acts 8:4-40. Ask yourself three questions: How do I see myself in this story? What is this story teaching me about myself? So what?

WEEKEND PRACTICE
Make a Plan

As you reflect on the work of Christ in your life, think about Jesus as a carpenter partnering with you in your life's work. Consider the creation stories in Genesis and God's creative power in you to bring order where there is chaos and creativity and life where none exists. Consider withstanding the short-term questions and uncertainties of people around you in order to withstand the longer-term floods. Keep knocking at doors until you find connection and peace. Do not fear acting on what you already know, what God has already shown you.

Begin by journaling about what a miracle of faith would look like for you. Be very specific and detailed about what your life of faith would look like if a miracle occurred. If a miracle in your faith journey happened tonight while you were sleeping, and you woke up in the morning to find that the miracle had indeed occurred, what would be the first thing you'd notice? What would you be doing differently? How would you spend your time? With whom would you spend the most time? What would other people in your life see you doing differently? Be as detailed as you possibly can in the description of your spiritual miracle. Spend at least thirty minutes describing and/or envisioning your spiritual miracle. Try to envision a day-to-day experience rather than any particular event or outcome. Focus on the behaviors and feelings that would be present, rather than on those that would not be present. For example, "I'd wake up and spend time in prayer and eat a filling, enjoyable breakfast," rather than "I wouldn't have headaches anymore."

Then, consider which parts of your miracle are already occurring. Which parts of your miracle involve specific, doable behaviors that you are already doing sometimes? What would it take for you do those behaviors a little bit more often? Make an action plan based on the reflections in week six. If it's helpful to you, follow this format:

	Your personal goal	A specific action step you will take this week
Ways I can build a partnership with Jesus		
Ways I can create order, beauty, and life		
Ways I am investing in long-term protection from the floodwaters of life		
Ways I can keep knocking on doors and connecting with others		
Ways I can take action in the face of uncertainty		

Miracles occur every day if we are willing to be aware of them. Focus on what yours will be, and make them happen. Get help and support, since we all need it.

CONCLUSION

Before writing this book I only wrote in ways that felt safely contained or safely intellectualized. My primary outlet for writing is through private diaries and journals I've kept since elementary school. Journaling fulfills my desire to write with no accountability for grammar or appropriateness of content. My journal writing is as unfiltered as it is unshared. My shared writing is mostly in the form of academic papers and articles, which are much more within my comfort zone of knowledge, skill, and confidence. If you look up my academic publications, you'll recognize topics important to me like eating disorder treatment, faith, college adjustment, and health. But if you've made it this far through *Revealed*, you don't just know what topics interest me. You've gotten to know *me*.

When I began writing a blog, I took more risks and began to dip my toe into the vulnerable waters of sharing myself through writing. This book has taken me even further beyond my comfort zone. Through my personal therapy, my relationships, and my writing, I am learning again that tapping into the most vulnerable, anxiety-producing places of myself allows me not only to move deeper into a more honest relationship with God, but also to engage more meaningfully with other people. When we assess honestly our spiritual and emotional states, we need not expend so much energy minimizing or avoiding them. We can enter more deeply into both pain and joy with the assurance of God's love and presence. Fear and struggle continue to show up, but so does God.

While I was writing this book and working through questions about how much of my personal journey to share, I had a dream that I was in a room with several large, wooden doors. Each door had a complicated sets of locks, and once I managed to secure one, another would come loose. No matter what I did, the doors would not stay locked. They kept rattling and coming unfastened. I began to prepare to protect myself against what might be on the other side. Then a friend approached me and gently urged me to let go. She told me that God wants me to play an active role in my life. I felt a wave of reassurance, and I knew that I could release my efforts to put so many defenses in place. I felt like I had that evening during college when I spoke the truth about my thorns.

My dream reminds me that we can find truth in everyday experiences and that relationships help us heal and step forward in faith.

Our path of self-awareness and its vacillating journey between baseline plateaus, crises of faith, and spiritual highs can be daunting and uncertain. It can feel a lot like trying to fasten locks on doors in an attempt to feel safe and secure: repetitive, tiring, complex, and frustrating. In those times, we can go to the Bible and find reassurance of God's loving presence. Any given moment may be a time to pause in silence, to weep, or to engage more actively in completing the work that God has begun.

On the last morning of a long weekend away with Dusty, Carlson, Caleb, and Zach, I enjoyed a few extra moments of rest while the thick curtains blocked out the morning light. Zach arose first, grasped the rod on the curtains, and pulled them open, revealing a burst of light into the room. It took my eyes a few moments to adjust, and I would have preferred the familiarity of the darkness for a while longer. Sometimes letting in the light is uncomfortable and stirs us from a place we'd prefer to leave undisturbed. It would be easier to keep the curtains closed and stay in our comfortable but familiar darkness. But it's essential in our faith journey that we allow the light to come in even when we are uncomfortable. The Bible reminds us that Jesus weeps with us in our pain when we would rather avoid or minimize it. God's love illuminates our discomfort and brings healing. The Bible teaches us that truth shows up through familiar people and unexpected places in our lives. The Bible also prompts us to look for joy as we play, flow, and spar together.

Finally, the Bible points us toward what is ahead. During this journey through some of the Bible's stories, I hope you've gained a better understanding of yourself. Reflect on the three questions that you identified at the beginning of this study. What did the Bible teach you regarding your questions? What did the Bible teach you about yourself? Where did you find yourself in the stories of the Bible?

Continue to revisit what you've learned about yourself from the Bible. When you revisit these and other familiar stories at different times in your life, different truths may stand out to you. You may continue to find yourself in different characters in the narratives, in different nuances of the stories, and in stories with which you've never self-identified before. Anytime you read a story from the Bible, you can ask yourself where you are in the story and how it pertains to your life with God and your loved ones. We can come back to the Bible at each stage of life, continue to explore our relationship to its stories and truths, and keep finding ourselves in it together.

Facilitator's Guide

This guide offers a structure for the group facilitator to follow each week. The facilitator can be one person or a different group member each week. For a more robust version of the guide with extra tips for facilitators, please visit http://www.angelaschaffnerphd.com/?page_id=25. For a ninety-minute meeting, I suggest the following schedule:

Informal social time together (15 minutes): The facilitator should be sure all group members have met one another and introduce any guests at each meeting.

Opening prayer and review of main points (5 minutes): Begin by spending time in prayer asking God to lead your group's discussion and reveal what group members may need to learn about themselves from the Bible stories. Ask one group member to describe briefly the week's main topics.

Discuss the week's reading (40 minutes): Allow the discussion questions to prompt and guide your conversation, and allow the conversation to flow naturally. Keep the discussion on-topic and make space for all group members to participate in the conversation.

Process the practice (15 minutes): Discuss the weekend practice and members' experiences with it. Highlight and encourage group members to participate in the takeaway challenge as they read next week's reflections.

Prayer requests and closing prayer (15 minutes): Allow time for each group member to share prayer requests. Consider having someone record these requests and email them to group members after the meeting. Read the suggested Psalm or another scripture passage and close in prayer.

Introduction

Opening Prayer

Loving God, we come to you with questions about ourselves, as works in progress. Provide the courage we need to face ourselves with self-reflective honesty and compassion and to encourage one another to navigate our questions together as we seek your love and truth in the Bible. Amen.

Discussion Questions

1. How have you approached and used the Bible over different periods of your life (childhood, adolescence, adulthood)?
2. What do you associate with the Bible in a positive way? in a negative way? What are your overall feelings toward the Bible?
3. How could you approach the Bible as if it were a person?
4. In what ways would you like to approach the Bible during this study? How are these different from your previous ways of approaching the Bible?
5. How do you relate to Noah? What are the floods in your life? What are you building that is meaningful to you? What would you like to build in preparation for the storms that may be ahead of you?

Process the Practice

Ask group members to share, as they are comfortable, any of the three questions about themselves that they identified. Allow them to share more about where the questions come from and what they are hoping to get from the study. Takeaway Challenge: Read your three questions about yourself daily this week. When you reflect on your questions, pray for God's guidance and provision of peace during the self-reflective work you will do on your journey through this study. Pick any passage of scripture to read each day, and practice maintaining an open mind and considering that the Bible can teach you something about yourself. If you have trouble choosing a passage, try Psalm 23. Write down any insights you have.

Prayer Requests and Closing Prayer (Psalm 1)

Week One: What You Already Have

Opening Prayer

Loving God, you are present in our daily lives, and you know the areas of our hearts where we feel pain and suffering. Show us how to seek healing in the places in our hearts that reflect your truth. Help us receive your guidance. Amen.

Discussion Questions

1. How do you seek to climb higher in measures of wealth, status, achievement, or appearance? What is your "tree?" How do you feel Jesus calling you to "come down"?

2. In 1 Samuel 17, Saul's armor weighs down David and would prevent him from effectively facing Goliath. What "armor" weighs you down in the face of a current challenge?

3. In what ways might others experience your efforts to help them as a burden or hindrance?

4. In the parable of the good Samaritan, the priest and Levite recognized the traveler's suffering but walked right by on the other side of the road. When have you had that type of response to your own pain or suffering? What part of your internal life today would you rather not stop to address? What are you concerned may happen if you did stop to address it?

5. How did the Bible change your perspective on life this week? How can it help you to remember that we only see part of God's whole truth?

Process the Practice

Invite group members to read aloud their Modern Creeds. Note the similarities and differences in each creed. Discuss together what you see as common threads that tie the creeds together. Discuss individual differences as well. Takeaway Challenge: Read aloud your Modern Creed each morning in the coming week. Consider whether there is anything you notice happening differently in your day as a result of reading your creed.

Prayer Requests and Closing Prayer (Psalm 121)

Week Two: What to Do with Your Pain

Opening Prayer

God of our deserts, we attempt to exercise control over our schedules, our families, and other people. Remind us that your grace is sufficient to help us keep moving forward in spite of the thorns that may continue to pierce us. Teach us how to learn from them. Lead us in your ways with the loving support of other faithful believers. Amen.

Discussion Questions

1. In 2 Corinthians 12:6-10, Paul pleads for his thorns to be removed. In the reflection, the author identifies her thorns of self-doubt and self-criticism. What are your thorns?
2. Ask one participant to read aloud the story of David and Bathsheba (2 Samuel 11). Share a time when you found yourself on a "rooftop of discontent." How did you respond to your discontent?
3. What seduces you? How do you allow your seductions to lead you toward a corner that may result in pain or regret?
4. What is an example in your life, or the life of someone close to you, of something good that you have hoped and prayed for, but has not yet come to pass? How do you make sense of where you are in this process? How do you continue to hope and pray for this good thing?
5. Consider a time when you struggled to understand the events of your life. Recall how you felt Jesus' presence or absence. How can you embrace the idea of Jesus weeping with you through difficult events in the future?

Process the Practice

Invite members to share their experiences with journaling. Encourage those who completed a time line to share one or two things they noticed if they are comfortable doing so. Discuss experiences of spiritual comfort during painful times. Takeaway Challenge: In your journal, list three things for which you are thankful each day. Note whether any of your impulsive behaviors shift as a result.

Prayer Requests and Closing Prayer (Psalm 69)

Week Three: Where You Find Truth

Opening Prayer

Loving God, you provide peace amid our trials. Help us to listen for your peace and guidance through other people and our own emotional experiences, even in unexpected places. Thank you for guiding us toward truth in the ways we need to hear it. Amen.

Discussion Questions

1. What is it like for you to think of God as a place?
2. Which places best represent God to you? Describe the ways those places help you envision, experience, and understand God.
3. Where are your unexpected sources of truth? How do you listen for truth in everyday, unexpected places? How can you listen to parts of yourself that you readily seek to silence?
4. How readily do you acknowledge the limits to your own wisdom?
5. How much do you tend to worry? What steps can you take to be less worried and more secure in the true fear of God?

Process the Practice

Invite group members to describe their sacred spaces. Allow some time for everyone to share how they chose their sacred spaces and how creating a sacred space has been helpful. Takeaway Challenge: For one day this coming week, approach every place, person, and experience you have as an opportunity to learn something from God. At the end of the day, write down what you learn in your journal.

Prayer Requests and Closing Prayer (Psalm 139:1-12)

Week Four: How Your Relationships Heal

Opening Prayer

Lord of the whole body, when we face challenges, help us heal through one another's supportive, silent presence. Help us love ourselves as our neighbors and our neighbors as ourselves. Show us how our individual gifts fit into a bigger picture of collective gifts within our church and community. Help us move forward with renewed hearts today. Amen.

Discussion Questions

1. Recall a time when you shared in Job's pain in some way. How did your loved ones help you through that time? How do you try to help others make sense of pain?

2. Which comes easier to you, loving yourself or loving others? How does one affect the other?

3. Identify one relational pattern (keeping the peace, rescuing others, criticizing others, avoiding conflict, etc.) that you tend to repeat, even when it is not in your best interest. What can you do differently to try to break one of those patterns and move forward in a relationship in a more positive way?

4. Have every group member find a piece of blank paper and create two columns. Choose one participant to read Proverbs 31:10-31 aloud very slowly. As the rest of the group listens, ask group members to jot down characteristics of the Proverbs 31 woman that they embody in the first column. In the second column, group members should jot down characteristics with which they struggle. Reflect aloud on qualities you embody and those with which you tend to struggle. Point out characteristics in each other that you see as strengths, and begin to consider the passage as a group challenge rather than an individual challenge.

5. Name one instance in your life where you need to drop a stone of accusation. How can focusing on our common need for God help you with this goal?

Process the Weekend Practice

Ask group members to share what they learned through their practices of forgiveness toward themselves and toward another person. Emphasize the difference between forgiveness (an individual choice and practice) and reconciliation (a practice for two or more people who work together to repair a relationship). Takeaway Challenge: Write on one stone some of the sins you do not struggle with much but tend to evaluate in other people. On the other, write some of your own sins, the ones that are most painful to bring to mind, that you know caused pain in your life and/or the lives of others. Then visit a nearby pond, lake, or stream. Drop the stones of accusation you tend to carry toward others and toward yourself. Drop the stones into the water, and pray that you'll remain mindful of your shared humanity and treat yourself and others with the compassion of Jesus.

Prayer Requests and Closing Prayer (Psalm 32)

Week Five: Why Your Faith Needs Fun

Opening Prayer

Dear God, help us carve out time to be with you and others in enjoyable ways. Remind us that conflict is part of every growing relationship, including our relationship with you. Help us return to you and remain in you. Amen.

Discussion Questions

1. Name an adult you know with a carefree sense of play. What can you learn from the person? What one step can you take to bring more play into your life?
2. Imagine the daily life of Jesus' first disciples. When do you think the disciples experienced flow?
3. When have you readily entered conflict? When do you shy away from it? What has healthy conflict looked like in your relationships? How could your conflicts be healthier?
4. What are some ways you "visit" excitement? How do you establish and return to a steady, calm, go-to spiritual place?
5. How can your healthiest intimate relationships help you better understand your relationship with God?

Process the Practice

Discuss how much time and energy group members currently devote to play. Ask them to share their experiences of play in the past week. Discuss the connection between the ways they have enjoyed play in the past and the activities they chose for the weekend practice. Takeaway Challenge: Beginning this week, carve out some weekly time to devote to play. Experiment with at least three different ways of experiencing play in the coming month, and note how your experience of faith changes as a result of giving yourself permission to play.

Prayer Requests and Closing Prayer (Psalm 33)

Week Six: What Is Next for You

Opening Prayer

Dear Jesus, you know our past and present, and you lead us into our future. Grant us insight and persistence as we move forward in our lives as works in progress. Open our eyes to miracles that are already occurring in our lives. Amen.

Discussion Questions

1. What internal renovations are you pursuing or do you want to pursue? How might you experience Christ coming alongside you with compassion and understanding as you work on internal vulnerabilities and challenges?
2. Which developmental stage of Creation do you identify with at this point in your life?
3. What are your best emotional coping skills? Consider skills that involve others as well as skills that you use when you are alone. How can you hone your skills so that they represent an ark that can withstand emotional floods?
4. Recall a time when you felt as though you were knocking on doors and persistence was required to meet your goal. How did it turn out?
5. What steps can you take this week to act in the face of the unknown and to create more of what you want in your life?

Process the Practice

Invite group members to share the miracles they envisioned in their faith journeys. Encourage them to identify ways that small pieces of their miracles may already be occurring. Then invite group members to share the ways they feel challenged to act in their lives of faith. Takeaway Challenge: Encourage group members to schedule a time to meet again in about a month to check in with one another about how they are doing with their plans and how they have continued to reflect on this study. This can be a more casual, social event or a formal meeting similar to those you've had thus far.

Prayer Requests and Closing Prayer (Psalm 23)

NOTES

Week One: What You Already Have

Come Down

1. William Barclay, *The Gospel of Luke* (Louisville, KY: Westminster John Knox Press, 2001), 5-6, 276–79.

Your Own Good Samaritan

1. William Barclay, *The Gospel of Luke* (Louisville, KY: Westminster John Knox Press, 2001), 164–67.
2. Sigmund Freud, *The Ego and the Id*, ed. James Strachey, trans. Joan Riviere (New York: W. W. Norton & Company, 1960), 16–17.
3. Eric Berne, *Games People Play: The Basic Handbook of Transactional Analysis* (Mass Market Paperback, 1969), 11–12.

Mirror, Mirror

1. Kathy Kater, *Healthy Bodies: Teaching Kids What They Need to Know; A Comprehensive Curriculum to Address Body Image, Eating, Fitness, and Weight Concerns in Today's Challenging Environment* (New York: Body Image Health, 2012), 3:15.

Unrestricted

1. Ralph Carson, *The Brain Fix: What's the Matter with Your Gray Matter* (Deerfield Beach, FL: Health Communications, Inc., 2012), 246–56.
2. Ralph Carson, "The Healing Brain: Integrating 12 Steps, Positive Psychology, and Neurochemistry into a Model for Recovery" (presentation, 2nd National Conference on Trauma, Addictions, and Intimacy Disorders, Nashville, TN, May 2, 2015).

Week Two: What to Do with Your Pain

Weeping

1. Stephanie Zacharek, Eliana Dockterman, and Haley Sweetland Edwards, "The Silence Breakers: The Voices that Launched a Movement," *Time,* December 18, 2017.
2. "Victims of Rape and Sexual Violence," Rape, Abuse, & Incest National Network, https://www.rainn.org/statistics.

Week Three: Where You Find Truth

Kihaps

1. Michael Casey, *Sacred Reading: The Ancient Art of* Lectio Divina (Liguori, MO: Liguori/Triumph, 1995), 80–87.

Fear

1. Leslie S. Greenberg, and Paivio, Sandra C. *Working with Emotions in Psychotherapy* (New York: Guilford, 1997), 194–203.
2. Gavin de Becker, *The Gift of Fear: Survival Signals That Protect Us from Violence* (New York: Dell Publishing, 1997), 299–303.

Week Four: How Your Relationships Heal

Silent Comfort

1. Debbara Dingman (conversation in therapy, 2005).

As Yourself

1. Henri Nouwen, *Spiritual Direction: Wisdom for the Long Walk of Faith* (New York: HarperCollins, 2006), 110–11.

Snapping the Bowstrings

1. Harville Hendrix, *Getting the Love You Want: A Guide for Couples, 20th Anniversary Edition* (New York: Holt, 2008), 38–45.
2. Rick Kilmer (personal communication during treatment team meetings at Atlanta Center for Eating Disorders, 2005–2017).

Weekend Practice: Forgiveness

1. Robert D. Enright, *The Forgiving Life: A Pathway to Overcoming Resentment and Creating a Legacy of Love* (Washington, D.C.: American Psychological Association, 2012), 4–7.

Week Five: Why Your Faith Needs Fun

Play

1. Michael Yogman, Andrew Garner, Jeffrey Hutchinson, Kathy Hirsh-Pasek, and Roberta Michnick Golinkoff, "The Power of Play: A Pediatric Role in Enhancing Development in Young Children," *Pediatrics* 142, no. 3 (September 2018): 1–16.
2. Stuart Brown, *Play: How It Shapes the Brain, Opens the Imagination, and Invigorates the Soul* (New York: Penguin, 2009), 125.

Flow

1. Mihaly Csikszentmihalyi, *Flow: The Psychology of Optimal Experience* (New York: HarperCollins, 1990), 41.

Remain in Me

1. John Gottman, *Why Marriages Succeed or Fail, and How You Can Make Yours Last* (New York: Simon & Schuster, 1994), 97-98.
2. Esther Perel, *The State of Affairs: Rethinking Infidelity* (New York: HarperCollins, 2017), 158–67.

Week Six: What Is Next for You

A Carpenter's Work

1. Steve de Shazer, *Putting Difference to Work* (New York: W.W. Norton & Company, Inc., 1991), 113.

Creating Faith

1. HarperCollins Study Bible (NRSV).

Withstanding the Floodwaters

1. Marsha Linehan, *Cognitive-Behavioral Treatment of Borderline Personality Disorder* (New York: The Guilford Press, 1993), 62.

Knock, Knock

1. James O. Prochaska and Carlo Diclemente, "Stages and Processes of Self-Change of Smoking: Toward an Integrative Model of Change," *Journal of Consulting and Clinical Psychology* 51, no. 3 (July 1983): 390–95.

Acting in the Unknown

1. Kenneth I. Pargament, Harold G. Koenig, & Lisa M. Perez, "The Many Methods of Religious Coping: Development and Validation of the RCOPE," *Journal of Clinical Psychology*, 56, no. 4: 522–25.
2. Steve de Shazer, *Putting Difference to Work* (New York: W.W. Norton & Company, Inc., 1991), 113–19.